Protecting Patron Privacy

Protecting Patron Privacy

Safe Practices for Public Computers

Matthew Beckstrom

Foreword by Barbara Jones

LIBRARIES UNLIMITED™
An Imprint of ABC-CLIO, LLC
Santa Barbara, California • Denver, Colorado

Library of Congress Cataloging-in-Publication Data

Beckstrom, Matthew.

Protecting patron privacy : safe practices for public computers / Matthew Beckstrom ; foreword by Barbara Jones.

pages   cm

Includes bibliographical references and index.

ISBN 978-1-61069-996-9 (pbk : alk. paper) — ISBN 978-1-61069-997-6 (ebook)   1. Public access computers in libraries—United States.   2. Internet access for library users—United States.   3. Privacy, Right of—United States.   4. Internet—Security measures.   5. Data protection.   I. Title.

Z678.93.P83B43   2015

025.50285--dc23   2015004049

ISBN: 978-1-61069-996-9
EISBN: 978-1-61069-997-6

19 18 17 16 15   1 2 3 4 5

This book is also available on the World Wide Web as an eBook.
Visit www.abc-clio.com for details.

Libraries Unlimited
An Imprint of ABC-CLIO, LLC

ABC-CLIO, LLC
130 Cremona Drive, P.O. Box 1911
Santa Barbara, California 93116-1911

This book is printed on acid-free paper ∞
Manufactured in the United States of America

Images of Microsoft products are used with permission from Microsoft.

Images of Google products and the Google logo are registered trademarks of Google Inc., used with permission.

This book is dedicated to my family.

Contents

Foreword

The past decade has witnessed a sea change in the way librarians view one of the profession's most time-honored ethical principles and legal mandates: privacy. Matt Beckstrom clearly brings the origins of library privacy best practices into the twenty-first century—from protecting the freedom to read books privately, to the understanding of how cookies function to invade that right. The same technology that creates our vibrant information society also has the potential to chill it.

This book is special because Beckstrom provides the mechanics of how the Internet works with servers, with the Web, with operating systems—and where potential privacy breaches lurk. How the Windows operating system protects some privacy but not all, and what librarians can do to improve patron privacy. I am delighted that finally we have a book that tells it in plain language for those among us who are not "techies." As Matt says: "Understanding how privacy is lost on the Internet is the first step to helping secure it." And he tells us how to educate library staff and patrons to ensure the best possible privacy protection.

This book gives an excellent account of how libraries take the idealism of the *Code of Ethics* and the *Library Bill of Rights* and tells librarians and patrons how to take action to make it real. The economic pressure on governments and business to collect big data for economic gain is tremendous. At the same time, legislatures and the courts are responding to public pressure to protect our privacy. This dynamic environment means that all library workers and advocates need to be current on the impact of privacy on libraries. This book does that. In addition, Beckstrom cites the American Library Association frequently. The Office for Intellectual Freedom maintains a website: www.chooseprivacyweek .org. It also continues to monitor state library privacy legislation, which has taken some positive steps to include e-privacy. And the IFC Privacy Subcommittee welcomes member involvement.

Constantly updated information—along with this book—provide practitioners, decision makers, and the public the tools to choose privacy in our nation's libraries.

Barbara M. Jones
Director, Office for Intellectual Freedom
American Library Association

CHAPTER 1

Privacy and How It Is Lost

Privacy

Libraries and Privacy

Privacy is important to everyone. Privacy is something we have come to expect in certain situations, and when it is taken away from us or infringed in some way, we want it back. Imagine sitting in a library reading a book, and someone comes over and leans over your shoulder to see what you are reading. Imagine browsing the bookshelves at the library for books on dieting and having someone following you around trying to sell you diet food. What if an FBI agent was sitting with you, recording your conversation with your mother? We naturally have boundaries with other human beings, and respecting those boundaries is part of a civilized society. What if these same situations happened to you on the Internet? This is what is going on now with the growth and expanded use of the Internet. Companies are recording what we watch and read. Advertisers are recording our behavior and targeting us to make money. Governments are recording and saving everything we do on the Internet. The Internet has also become a breeding ground for individuals attempting to steal personal information or attack computers. We are losing our privacy on the Internet.

Why do we want privacy on the Internet? Should we expect to have any privacy when using the Internet? As mentioned before, it is upsetting to have someone constantly watching what you are doing, especially if they are recording it and using it in ways you have no control over. As we use the Internet, we should be able to control, as best we can, what people and companies see and record us doing.

Libraries have been providing their patrons with a certain level of privacy for many years. It is an official and basic right that libraries grant to their patrons. Just as patients consider their medical records to be private, library patrons expect that their right to view materials and services provided by the library comes with a certain level of privacy regarding what materials or services they have used. In 1939 the American Library Association (ALA) provided a *Code of Ethics for Librarians* that, in part, affirmed the "librarian's obligation to treat as confidential any private information obtained through contact with library patrons" (American Library Association, 1939). This affirmation obviously was in reference to traditional library services including material checkouts and facility use, but in more recent years it has been extended to include electronic access by patrons as well. The current version of the *Code of Ethics*, last amended in 2008, adds "with respect to information sought or received and resources consulted, borrowed, acquired or transmitted." The American Library Association also has published a *Library Bill of Rights* that many libraries follow. The *Library Bill of Rights* states that library users should have free access to all library resources, and that libraries should resist abridgment of free expression and free access to ideas (American Library Association, 1939). The Internet is treated by libraries the same as any collection and is considered part of the resources that they offer. These basic rights granted to library users for access to library resources naturally and rightly extend to the Internet.

Many states ensure privacy rights that cover how patrons utilize the library. Ten states offer privacy rights to their citizens in their state constitutions. The constitutions of Alaska, Arizona, California, Florida, Hawaii, Illinois, Louisiana, Montana, South Carolina, and Washington all have sections devoted to privacy. Forty-eight of the fifty states have laws regarding patrons' rights regarding use of public library materials and services. These laws grant library users the right to request and use library materials and services without having that use be made public, without a legal request from a court.

Most public libraries offer some form of Internet access to their patrons. A 2010 study by the Bill and Melinda Gates Foundation and the Institute of Museum and Library Services found that nearly every public library in the United States offers Internet-accessible terminals to their users. Patron use public terminals for a variety of reasons including job hunting, social connections, education, personal wellness, and research. If a library patron checks out a series of books on a personal subject such as pregnancy, they do not expect that those checkouts will be advertised to large retailers. If that same patron used the Internet at the public library and searched for information regarding pregnancy, could not the library attempt to provide a certain level of privacy to the patron regarding those searches?

However, recent news has shown that Internet users have less privacy than they may have thought. In May 2014, Edward Snowden, a contractor for the National Security Agency (NSA), released a series of top-secret NSA documents showing a widespread monitoring program by the NSA and several other foreign security agencies. Snowden documented a variety of government monitoring activities including the use of cookies to track users around the Internet the same way that advertisers use cookies to track users. The Snowden releases also revealed an NSA program called PRISM—a monitoring and data collection service conducted by the NSA. With this program, the NSA collects Internet-based communication from online companies like Google and Yahoo. The data is gathered and stored by the NSA. The data can then be searched for keywords authorized by a court and turned over to the NSA. For months after his initial leak, Edward Snowden continued to release documents showing Internet-based spying by the NSA and other governments, much to the shock and consternation of the public.

Some libraries have started to be more proactive in ensuring Internet privacy to their users. A few public libraries in Massachusetts have even started an all-out campaign to promote Internet privacy. In partnership with the American Civil Liberties Union of Massachusetts, they have created training programs and brochures, and installed privacy tools on public computers in an effort to raise awareness to library users of the importance of online privacy and to protect their patrons' privacy when using public computers.

In this book I will discuss the ways that privacy is lost on the Internet and show practical ways that privacy for library patrons can be protected. I talk about procedural changes that staff can make to reduce the amount of data that is stored about users. I will show changes that can be made to networks, network devices, physical spaces, Microsoft Windows, and Internet browsers to promote privacy. I will give some changes that can be made to library policies as they relate to patron privacy, and I will give some starting points for educational classes for patrons so they can be more aware of their own privacy on the Internet. It is meant to be a starting point, to get you started on understanding the complicated subject of privacy on the Internet. Many of the discussions on procedures, training, and policies should be the beginning to an entire organization-wide review of how the library handles privacy on the Internet for their patrons.

This book is aimed at libraries and librarians. It is targeted to any library that wants to do more to protect the privacy of their users on the Internet. While the focus of this book is more for public libraries, much of the practical advice would be useful to academic and school libraries. Academic and school libraries will have more problems implementing some of the policy and procedural changes since school districts work under different laws and regulations than public libraries. Much of the advice on educational classes and software advice on Windows and browsers may apply to school and academic libraries.

Privacy on the Internet

There is no way to guarantee that Internet use at the library will remain private. There are just too many ways for someone to lose their privacy, and too many ways for the advertisers, governments, and hackers on the Internet to steal that privacy. It seems as if every day, new ways to track people are unveiled. The best we can hope for is to minimize the risk that patrons take when using the computers in our libraries, and to educate them about the threats to privacy that exist on the Internet.

Understanding how privacy is lost on the Internet is the first step to helping secure it. The Internet is a very social form of communication. Not social in the way of Facebook or YouTube, but social in that the communications we send out over it are very public and easily listened to. Our communications are easy to watch, track, and monitor. These features were designed not to enable others to steal private information, but to make the Internet more usable and user-friendly. In the early days of the Internet, users wanted to share information and be social; privacy was not a major concern. Users today still want to share information and be social, but since we live more of our lives online, we also expect a certain level of privacy. As time passes, the Internet is used more and more for personal or private communications like banking and other financial transactions, school, private communication with loved ones, and personal research on private topics. Meanwhile, the Internet has become a much larger resource for advertisers, corporations, governments, and hackers. So it only makes sense that they would do what they can to exploit the social nature of the Web for their own purposes. With some basic education of library patrons, some changes to the way libraries offer public computers, policy and procedural changes, network and workstation changes, and some applications that we can install for patrons to use, we can help to provide a safer and more private Internet experience for our users.

How Is Privacy Lost on the Internet?

IP Address

Any device that is connected to the Internet is broadcasting a variety of information about itself, its connection, and the user to remote servers and sites. This information includes what operating system the user is using, what browser and browser version they are using, and what their Internet connection is. This behavior is expected and is useful for proper communication. Communication between devices on the Internet is made more efficient and allows a more enriching experience for the users when basic information about the devices and people using them is shared between devices. When a client connects to a server, the server can tailor the experience for the user based on their Internet connection or their browser type. Even though the behavior is expected to a degree, it can intrude too much on a user's privacy, often without their knowledge. Website operators can collect and store that data and use it to identify the user, or they can sell it to advertisers to make money.

Every device on the Internet has a unique number called an IP address. IP stands for Internet Protocol. IP is the form of communication that devices use when talking to each other. When a computer or device is connected to the Internet, it is constantly using its IP address to communicate, because every server it connects to must know its IP address in order to respond to it. In many networks, a system called Network Address Translation or NAT is used to connect devices to the Internet. Basically, NAT is a system that allows many devices on a network to share one Internet IP address. For example, your library may use NAT to allow all the staff computers to connect to the Internet using the same IP address. Each computer on the network is given a special IP address that is only good on that network. When that device communicates on the local network, it uses this special or private IP address. When that device wants to communicate on the Internet, the firewall translates the device's private IP address to a publicly available IP address that works on the Internet. Each device on the private network would use the same public IP address on the Internet. For the return communication, the firewall would translate the public IP communication back to the private IP for each device. Using this NAT system is useful to protect privacy, but only for the IP address. Devices also broadcast a wealth of other information that servers read like their operating system, the browser type and version, and what plug-ins are installed on the browser.

Client Information

When a connection is made between devices on the Internet like a public computer in a library and a remote website like www.ala.org, the public computer or client computer shares its connection information with the remote website or server. This includes the device's IP address, what type of device it is, and what operating system it is using (computer, PC, Mac, Android, etc.), as well as what type and version of browser it is using (Internet Explorer, Firefox, Chrome, etc.). This information is used by the server to provide a smoother experience, technically speaking, for the client. For example, when an Apple iPhone connects to an online merchant, it tells the server that it is an Apple iPhone 5 running IOS 7 and Safari version 4. The server then uses that information to send a particular type of website to the device that displays properly on the smaller screen of an iPhone and has the services available that will work on it.

But sites collect this data and keep it in logs. The logs are used to keep a history of what clients visited the sites, what pages they viewed, how long they were on the site, what they did on the site, where they came from, where they left the site, and what operating system, OS version, and browser they used. The site owners can then use that data for a variety of purposes. Most will use it to compile simple statistical data: how many visitors they had over a certain period of time, how many of each type of operating system or browser they used. They will also use it to understand how people use their site (e.g., what pages or links are most popular) so they can tailor it to operate better. Along with compiling statistical data, some sites give or sell their data to third-party companies or advertisers. Advertisers use the data to understand what types of people are visiting certain sites and what technology they use. Depending on what information the advertisers purchased from the site, they may also be able to know what the visitors did on the site including what products or pages they viewed, what they purchased, what they searched for, and how much time they spent looking at certain pages. This is useful for advertisers because it can help them create more effective advertising. For example, if a visitor is constantly viewing swimsuits on an online shopping site, the advertising on that page might start showing ads for suntan lotion, or suggest other types of beach wear. This information is shared across multiple sites. Furthermore, if many different sites each use the same advertising companies, the data they provide can be used on other sites. This allows a subscribing website to know what a visitor has viewed or purchased on other sites. They can then customize the viewer's experience based on their previous history.

This allows one online merchant to suggest swimwear or other beach products to the same visitor who was viewing swimsuits on a different site. This behavior is not always unwanted by users, and in fact can be quite useful and make the shopping experience for the end user more enriching. At the same time, this behavior is done without the knowledge of the users. They are not given the option to share their information with advertisers, nor with other sites.

Cookies

Sometimes when you visit certain websites, Internet servers store small files called cookies on the computer. These cookie files store information related to the session that the computer and the server are currently using. For example, when a user visits a library website that uses cookies, the server automatically puts a cookie on the user's computer that contains what time the user starting viewing the site, what pages they viewed, how long they were on the site, if they logged into the site or not, and what they clicked on while on the site. There are different types of cookies that sites use, depending on their need.

- **Session cookies**—A session cookie is one that is created when the user visits the site and remembers basic information about the user's visit. When the cookie is set, it is not given an expiration date, and typically it is stored in the computer's memory. When the user leaves the site or closes the browser, the session cookies are deleted from memory. Session cookies typically contain shopping cart information and browsing habits.

- **Persistent cookies**—A persistent cookie is given an expiration date when it is set. The expiration date is set by the server and can be almost any time period. When a persistent cookie is created, it is stored in a temporary file on the computer where the browser has access to them. Where cookies are stored depends on the browser. The cookie will remain in the temporary directory until the expiration date, or until the browser automatically or the user manually deletes it. When the user visits a site that already has a persistent cookie set, the server requests that cookie, and it will be loaded and sent to the server. Persistent cookies store more information about the user and their habits. For example, they store where the user came from (search engine or other sites), what they did on the site, what pages they viewed, what they clicked on, and how long they were on the site. Due to their persistent nature, they can also store user personalization settings like preferred language, site colors, or custom graphics or skins.

- **Third-party cookies**—A third-party cookie originates from a different site than the one being visited. For example, when you visit www.onlineseller.com, the site will likely contain information and images from advertisers. When the site sends this website data to you, it may contain cookies that originate from the advertisers, like www.onlineadvertiser.com. Since this cookie does not come directly from the site that you typed in (www.onlineseller.com), it is considered a third-party cookie. When you visit another site like www .alsoseller.com that also uses www.onlineadvertiser.com, the third-party cookie is loaded and all the information about your browsing habits from www.onlineseller.com is sent to the advertiser. Third-party cookies contain the same browsing habit information that persistent cookies contain. The biggest difference is that the information in a persistent cookie is only visible to the originating server, and the data in a third-party cookie is visible to the advertiser; it is used to create a browsing history for that user. The advertiser can then create specific ads for that particular user since they know what sites that user visited and what they did on those sites. Third-party cookies do not store specific identifiable information about the user, but based on the information that they do store, it is possible for an advertiser to create a rather specific profile about a particular user.

- **Supercookies**—A supercookie is a specialized type of regular cookie. They are put on the computer in the same manner by browsing sites that use supercookies, but they are usually installed using a different mechanism that puts them into different locations on the computer. Since they are not installed in the same way as regular cookies, they act outside of the usual restrictions placed on cookies in the browser preferences. So, if you configure your browser to block cookies, and then browse to a site that uses supercookies, it is still possible for that supercookie to be installed. One of the most common types of supercookie installed is the type with the Adobe Flash plug-in. Plug-ins are programs that are installed in a web browser and extend the functionality by adding new capabilities. Flash is a browser plug-in that enables website operators to use videos or graphics in an enriching way for the end user. Some media sites that offer videos for entertainment or news use Flash for their video feeds. When the video feed starts to play, the server will push down a supercookie to the client. Supercookies contain the same information as regular cookies, but they are able to gain additional information that regular cookies cannot access. In some situations, it is actually possible for supercookies to restore deleted regular cookies, or to create cookies based on the supercookie.

Beacons

A web beacon, or as they are sometimes called, a web bug, is a small file that is stored on a webpage and is downloaded with the page content when a user requests that page. Beacons are typically invisible one-pixel images that when activated send session information back to the server. In many ways, they are similar to cookies in that the information they request is the same. They gather the browser type and version, the operating system, the time and date of the transaction, and what content the user requested. And they also contain a unique tracking ID for each user so that the server can keep track of each user as they navigate the site.

Beacons are useful for site owners since they are easier to manage than user statistics and cookies. If a site owner has multiple sites on their servers, they can easily monitor and track users by using beacons. The data retrieved by a beacon is not clearable by the end user the way that a cookie is. Cookies can be deleted and the information contained in them lost, but when a beacon sends its information to the server, it is stored on the server.

Beacons are also used in email to track who opens a message and when. When an email is sent to users, the text of the message is embedded with a link to the beacon. Each beacon is identified using a unique identifier, so when the user opens the email and downloads the beacon, it reports back the unique identifier, and the email sender is aware of who opened that message and when. Many email applications today do not automatically load the image files embedded in emails in order to prevent this behavior from happening. If a user wants to download the graphics and the beacon, they have to click on a link to show the graphics.

Scripts/Social Networks

Social networks, such as Facebook, track users as they move around the Internet. Many site operators put "like" buttons on their webpages. These "like" buttons allow users to say that they like a particular website or document on a website. When a user visits a page that contains a script to a social network, that webserver tells the social network that a particular user visited that website, thus creating a script of the user's Internet movements. If the user happened to be logged into Facebook at the time they visited the page, then the visit to that page is logged with the user's Facebook profile.

Many other social networks (e.g., Twitter, Instagram) also use a script to place icons on websites. It is common to see a whole line of icons, each one from a different social network, and each one reporting back to their social network that a user just visited a certain website.

Public Computers

Public computers in libraries are accessible to many people, other patrons, and staff. During a typical single day, many people use or have access to the computers and could potentially view the information stored on the computers. Any browsing behavior, saved temporary files, cookies, saved passwords, browser bookmarks, and so on that are created by a previous user are potentially viewable by another user. For this reason, public computers in libraries are not private.

Placement of public computers also brings up privacy issues. If a public computer is located in a place where it is possible for another person to view what is on the screen, then the privacy of the patron next to them is inhibited. As discussed in chapter 2, public computer placement is a vital, but generally difficult, way to protect patron privacy.

Search Engines

Search engines like Google, Bing, and Yahoo comprise a vital part of the Internet. With the number of pages and sites available on the Internet, it is obvious that users need a way to locate the information they are looking for. Search engines on the Internet compile lists of pages and create indexes of keywords that a user can search for. Most modern search engines save searches that are performed by users. By doing this, the search engine can better tailor the results list to make it more useful for the user. For example, if you search for sunscreen on Google, then search for tanning, the Google search engine puts results that contain both those words in it toward the top of the results list. Google and other search engines also place customized ads on the search result pages, based on the search terms you searched for.

Some search engines also keep a history of the searches you perform. Depending on the search engine, if you have an account with the search engine and you are logged into it, it might keep a history of searches. Google, for instance, stores a history of search terms. You can view a list of your recent searches on Google if desired.

Those using the same public computer can easily see another person's searches. If one user uses Google to search the Internet, the next user who uses Google to search will have access to the search history of that user. The browser also keeps cached files of all the search pages, and these are visible to other users by viewing the history. When another user starts a search, Google will drop down a list of recently searched terms by other users. Other users could also open the browser history and see all the search pages previous users viewed. This will show a list of the search terms the previous user searched for and what links they clicked on. Browser history will also show search histories for other search engines.

Fingerprinting

Fingerprinting is another method that remote servers on the Internet can use to identify certain clients. When a client connects to a remote server, it gives that server all kinds of information including the browser, the browser version, the operating system, and much more information. By gathering all this information, a server can create a picture, or "fingerprint," of that client's attributes and use that to identify the client in future transactions.

Fingerprinting works even if a client disables or refuses cookies. The behavior of the browser when broadcasting specifics about itself is not dependent on cookie settings. Even though a fingerprint is created using information that the browser gives out all the time, useful fingerprinting requires the gathering of more specifics and parameters about a particular client. The more parameters the fingerprint contains, the more specific it is to a particular user. In order to gather a more specific fingerprint for a user, a server relies on other types of access to the client machine, typically gained through Java or some other client-side scripting language. Since Java is used extensively on the Internet, it is difficult to disable Java all the time to prevent fingerprinting.

Since fingerprinting works independently of the browser cookies and other common methods of tracking that are more specific to a particular user, it has a tendency to be more useful in tracking a particular computer instead of the user. In a public library setting, this is dangerous since many people will use the same computer every day. If a server was tracking a particular computer based on a fingerprint, then it would assume that every user on that computer was the same person. Any ads or other types of targeting advertising would be inaccurate and could potentially show the habits of a previous user. For example, if a user in the morning spent a lot of time searching for information and products on pregnancy and babies, the advertising networks could target baby or pregnancy–based ads at future users on the same computer.

Viruses and Spyware

Viruses and spyware are a common way for a user's private information and browsing habits to be shared and compromised on the Internet. When they attach themselves to a specific computer, some types of viruses can search the computer for personal information and send this out to unknown persons over the Internet. Some viruses can gather the email addresses from the user's email account and send copies of those to other people.

Spyware is a general term that is used to describe any application that is installed on the computer that attempts to steal the user's personal information or browsing habits. Spyware comes in many different formats including browser add-ons, free games or applications, or programs installed on the computer without the user's knowledge.

Often spyware gets onto a computer when the user sees an offer on a webpage for a free toolbar or browser plug-in that offers some service like easy access to email, specialized search box for a popular website, or some other type of online activity. When the user installs these browser plug-ins, they often start gathering personal information about the user including name, address, email address, or any other kind of information put into online forms; browsing habits, like what sites are visited, how long they were there, what they searched for; and other online behavior. Sometimes these plug-ins have the ability to gather passwords, usernames, credit card information, and other security credentials from the user. Once this information is gathered, it can be sent to a server on the Internet where that information is either used against the user such as in identity theft or credit card fraud, sold to advertisers for marketing purposes, or used to target specific websites or advertisements. After the toolbar or add-on is installed on the browser, it is used to target specific advertisements to the user. The user will then experience more pop-up windows, advertisements placed on pages, and even browser redirection. When the user searches for something and clicks on a link to visit that page, the spyware application can redirect that click to another page that is chosen by the spyware operator. Sometimes when the user types in a web address directly, the spyware application will redirect that to a different site that the spyware operator gets paid to show.

Spyware applications are usually packaged with another application like a free utility or game available on the Internet. Users may be offered a free disk check utility or a program to speed up their computer. When they download it and install it, they are also installing the spyware application that runs in the background of the computer and starts to gather personal information, browsing habits, and so on. Spyware often works the same way as browser plug-ins by redirecting search queries, offering advertising pop-ups, or placing ads directly on websites. In some cases the spyware also acts as a host to a spyware operator that uses the user's computer to send out viruses or spam messages. Obviously, this type of behavior is dangerous to the computer and could result in a reaction from the user's Internet provider, which may see large amounts of traffic coming from the user's computer and block it.

Some extreme forms of spyware, also called ransomware, attempt to take the user hostage by claiming that the computer has been infected with some kind of virus or by stating that the computer was used in a crime. The only way to "clean" the infected computer or to remove the possibility of it being used in a crime is to pay the ransomware application maker money. Of course, there is no horrible infection, other than the spyware itself, or evidence of the computer being used in a crime; it is all simply designed to steal money from the user. In recent years, there has been a rash of computers being encrypted with a very complex code that can only be decrypted by paying the ransom (Constantin, 2014). All the user's personal files are encrypted, and they cannot be decrypted without the key from the ransomware maker, after paying up to $500 or more using online currency.

There are many ways that privacy can be lost on the Internet. The client computer is constantly broadcasting information about itself—what browser it is using, what its IP address is, what operating system it is using, and what configuration the browser has. As you browse the Web, you are constantly picking up cookies that can be used to track your use of the Internet, where you go, what you do, and for how long. Some cookies are persistent and can continue to track your behavior even between sessions. Beacons located on websites or in email can also track your behavior. Remote servers can fingerprint you based on the unique settings on your computer and use that to keep traces on your movement on the Internet. Viruses and spyware are designed to steal your personal data.

What does this mean to our patrons? When patrons come into the library and use the public computer, they risk being tracked on the Internet and losing their privacy. Once libraries and librarians are aware of the ways that privacy can be lost on public computers, they can start to create procedures, policies, and education to help protect their patrons' privacy and to protect the patrons' use of the resources that the library provides. This is no different from checking out library books. The library does not allow advertisers to know what books a patron checks out. The library will not give out the personal private information of a patron's use of the library without a court order. Patrons should expect a certain level of privacy provided by the library.

The next chapter covers procedures that staff can take to help combat some of the ways privacy is lost. It also discusses library policy and education for patrons.

Bibliography

American Library Association. "Code of Ethics of the American Library Association." Accessed December 20, 2014, http://www.ala.org/advocacy/proethics/code ofethics/codeethics

American Library Association. "Library Bill of Rights." Accessed December 20, 2014, http://www.ala.org/advocacy/intfreedom/librarybill/

American Library Association. "1939 Code of Ethics for Librarians." Accessed December 20, 2014, http://www.ala.org/Template.cfm?Section=History1&Template =/ContentManagement/ContentDisplay.cfm&ContentID=8875

American Library Association. "State Privacy Laws Regarding Library Records." Accessed December 20, 2014, http://www.ala.org/advocacy/privacy confidentiality/privacy/stateprivacy

Bill and Melinda Gates Foundation. "Opportunity for All: How the American Public Benefits from Internet Access at U.S. Libraries." Accessed December 2014, https://docs.gatesfoundation.org/Documents/OpportunityForAll.pdf

Boingboing. "Radical Librarianship: How Ninja Librarians Are Ensuring Patrons' Electronic Privacy." Last modified September 13, 2014, http://boingboing .net/2014/09/13/radical-librarianship-how-nin.html

Constantin, Lucian. "CryptoWall Ransomware Held over 600K Computers Hostage, Encrypted 5 Billion Files." Last modified August 29, 2014, http:// www.pcworld.com/article/2600543/cryptowall-held-over -halfamillion-computers-hostage-encrypted-5-billion-files.html

Electronic Frontier Foundation. "The Web Bug FAQ." Accessed December 20, 2014, https://w2.eff.org/Privacy/Marketing/web_bug.html

Infosec Island. "Facebook "Like" Button = Privacy Violation + Security Risk." Last modified May 21, 2012, http://www.infosecisland.com/blogview/21386 -Facebook-Like-Button--Privacy-Violation--Security-Risk.html

Mashable. "Supercookies: What You Need to Know About the Web's Latest Tracking Device." Last modified September 2, 2011, http://mashable.com/2011/09/02 /supercookies-internet-privacy/

National Conference of State Legislatures. "Privacy Protections in State Constitutions." Last modified December 12, 2014, http://www.ncsl.org/research/telecommuni cations-and-information-technology/privacy-protections-in-state-constitutions .aspx

PC World. "CryptoWall Ransomware Held over 600K Computers Hostage, Encrypted 5 Billion Files." Last modified August 29, 2014, http://www.pcworld.com /article/2600543/cryptowall-held-over-halfamillion-computers-hostage -encrypted-5-billion-files.html

Pew Internet. "Anonymity, Privacy, and Security Online." Last modified September 5, 2013, http://www.pewinternet.org/2013/09/05/anonymity-privacy-and-security -online/

Washington Post. "NSA uses Google Cookies to Pinpoint Targets for Hacking." Last modified December 10, 2013, http://www.washingtonpost.com/blogs/the -switch/wp/2013/12/10/nsa-uses-google-cookies-to-pinpoint-targets-for -hacking/

CHAPTER 2

Staff Procedures and Policy

Staff Procedures and Policy

Staff Procedures

As you begin to understand patron privacy on the Internet, and what you can do to help protect it, it makes sense to start with the procedures libraries use. Libraries use a variety of systems like computer reservation systems, firewalls, and routers that track all usage. The first place you should start is with a review of those systems. Start by understanding what information you collect, how it is stored, and how it can be cleared. Create procedures for staff to regularly review those systems and clear all the personal information from them. This should be done with the assistance of the technology department of your library to make sure that any information in these systems that may be used for statistical purposes or for maintenance and tuning is not lost. Libraries operate using policies that define their actions and how they provide services. These policies should be updated to include Internet safety and privacy. New policies may need to be created to accommodate privacy concerns with the library website and the collection of data by other entities the library does business with.

On the public computers themselves, a lot of information is stored in many places and by many different applications. This stored information should be regularly reviewed and deleted when possible.

Patron Usage Logs

When patrons use a computer or other technology in the library, they create a series of logs that document their usage of that technology. If they use a public computer, they may have to reserve that computer with their library card, or use some form of identification. While they are using the computer, they are also leaving traces of their usage on the computer including history logs, temporary files, and other logs. If they check out a computer or tablet, once again they usually have to use their library card or some other form of identification. Wireless networks also create usage logs of particular devices, including the times the users connect, what sites they access, and how much data they use. These types of logs are not dangerous in and of themselves and are quite useful for a variety of reasons. Computer usage logs are used to show technology usage at the library, which is useful in determining service levels and providing the library with the information that helps them determine if they need more or fewer computers, or how to allocate resources more efficiently. In fact, many states have requirements for libraries to report technology usage. Without usage logs, it would be impossible for the library to accurately report usage. These logs reveal personally identifiable information that lists what devices the patrons used, when, and in some cases, what they did. This information could be obtained by law enforcement agencies with a court order. The library can help protect patrons' privacy by creating procedures to clear the usage of these devices.

If a law enforcement agency requests information from a library with a court order, it is typically in response to a legal issue. If the library can comply and provide information to assist law enforcement, then they will supply all the records that are requested. If law enforcement is asking for firewall logs, for example, they will get all the logs from the firewall that will include the connection information for all the devices on the network. This could include information about connections and usage that does not relate to the legal issue. If a computer is requested, then all the information on the computer is supplied including all the records of previous users on the computer. This is not meant to be an intentional block to the courts to supply information. Libraries should provide as much information as they can to prevent laws from being broken, but at the same time, they must provide a level of privacy and security for their patrons. With electronic records on computers, firewalls, and other electronic devices, it is difficult to separate the uses from one user to the next.

According to a recent survey by the American Library Association, 99 percent of public libraries provide access to public computers, and almost 100 percent of public libraries provide Internet access to patrons (American Library Association, 2012). Public computer and Internet access is a popular service in libraries; many libraries have implemented reservation systems to help them manage computer usage.

These systems usually link to the library automation system, confirming that the patron has a library card, and that the card is valid. When the patron scans the library card at a public computer, the system queries the automation system. Sometimes when the reservation system queries the automation system, it actually creates an entry or a log on the automation system that shows the patron reserved a computer. The reservation systems also have logs that they keep in order to troubleshoot issues or locate problems with the system. These logs have the date and time of the reservation, information about the patron, and depending on the configuration, could include the patron's name and library card number, what computer they used, and for how long. Depending on the reservation system, the system may also record whether the patron used a filtered computer or an unfiltered computer.

These logs do not necessarily show what the patron did on the computer and do not show what sites the patron visited, but they do show that the patron used the computer, what computer they used, and what time they used the computer. With this information and other stored information on the computer including browser history and temporary Internet files, it is possible for someone to find out who visited a particular website during a given time period. The computer itself may contain logs showing what sites were visited, and the Internet provider might have logs showing what Internet sites were visited on a specific computer. It would then just take the logs from the reservation record or automation system to identify who did it.

Most reservation systems have a feature that allows you to clear the logs. The logs can be cleared on a daily or weekly schedule. They would still maintain basic information about the session like the time the computer was reserved, how long it was used for, and other session-related information that the library could use for statistical purposes. Most libraries keep statistics of how many times the public computers are used and do not want to lose those numbers. The same would go for reservation systems that query the automation system. If the reservation system makes a change to the patron account in order to indicate that the patron used a computer, you can purge that change daily or weekly, unless the session information is not recorded in the first place. At the least, the system can maintain that the patron used a computer, but not which one, or what time.

Network firewalls also maintain logs of all the traffic that passes through them. In most cases, the data they collect includes the IP address and sites visited by each computer on the network. Network administrators use these logs for a variety of purposes, including network monitoring, protecting the network against security breaches and threats, and network maintenance. Network monitoring includes checking that the firewall traffic maintains consistency with network services. If a firewall becomes overloaded, the administrator can reroute traffic to better handle the loads. Monitoring network traffic accomplishes the same task, but could also be used for Internet filtering. Using firewall logs is very helpful in protecting the network from unwelcome intrusions or other threats. The administrator uses a log viewer or an automated system to determine if an IP address on the network is infected with a virus or is being used to send out spam or some other type of attack.

So, firewall logs are extremely useful and are necessary to protect the integrity of the network, but like automated systems, they can also be cleared on a regular basis to protect the privacy of the public computers. Depending on the brand of the firewall, it is even possible to clear specific IP addresses from the logs while maintaining other IP addresses in the logs. Clearing the logs of the firewall should be done as frequently as possible. Once again, working with the network administrator to determine the frequency of log clearing, a schedule should be determined.

Clearing Computer Records

There are many types of records and logs that are kept on a computer while a patron is browsing the Internet. Many of these logs and records remain on the computer after the patron finishes browsing and closes the browser; many can be used to identify the patron and where they went on the Internet, whether to other computer users or to specific Internet sites.

Internet Explorer History Settings

Internet browsers, such as Internet Explorer and Firefox, keep histories of all the sites visited. They do this to help users remember what sites they visited and when, in case they want to return to those sites. Browsers also temporarily keep copies of all the files that are downloaded by the browser. These temporary files include the text on the page and all the images; they are kept and identified by the site they came from. Temporary files are useful when browsing. When you click on the back button on the browser, it will quickly load the files from the computer instead of slowly reloading them from the server. This makes browsing the Internet faster and more efficient.

However, if other computer users access these files, they can potentially see what websites and webpages the previous users visited, and when.

Another feature of Internet browsers is allowing users to save their login credentials. This happens when a user logs onto a site with a username and password. While this feature is useful for personal computers, saving users from remembering or constantly looking up the information, for public computers, it is dangerous because it allows any user of the computer to log into secure sites as another user. For example, if a patron using a public computer logs into their email account and allows the computer to save the username and password, the next user to use that computer would be prompted to log into the same email account as the previous user if they visited the same site.

Thankfully, all these types of files that are stored by browsers can be disabled and cleared.

Configuring Internet Explorer

In Internet Explorer, you can view browsing history by clicking on the bookmarks and history icon on the toolbar, then clicking on the History tab.

Once inside the History tab, you will see the history of all the sites visited, sorted by the date. You can clear individual items by right clicking on them and choosing Delete.

Internet Explorer History

You can also clear all the history for Internet Explorer by clicking on the menu gear, going to Internet Options, then choosing Delete in the browsing history section.

Choosing this option allows you to clear more than just the browsing history. You can also clear the temporary Internet files, cookies data, saved passwords, and download history. In addition, you can turn off the ability of Internet Explorer to keep a history of sites visited.

Internet Explorer Options

1. Click on the menu gear, then on Internet options.

2. In the browsing history area, click on the Settings button.

3. Click on the History tab at the top and set the number of days you want Internet Explorer to keep a history. The default is 20 days. If you want to disable the feature, set it to 0.

Internet Explorer by default keeps temporary Internet files for all sites that are visited. Check the temporary files settings by clicking on the menu gear, then on Internet Options. On the general page, click on the Delete button to choose what temporary files to delete. Newer versions of Internet Explorer allow you to delete the temporary Internet files, but by default it will not delete files that are set as favorites in Internet Explorer. Since a patron could set a particular site as a favorite, it is quite possible that the temporary files will remain unless you uncheck this option.

Internet Explorer has several options to help you manage temporary Internet files. You can access these options by clicking on the menu gear, then clicking on Internet Options. On the advanced page, scroll down in the list until you find the security section. Checking the box next to the option "Empty temporary Internet files folder when browser is closed" will automatically delete all the files in the temporary Internet files directory when the browser is closed. You will also see an option to not save any files from encrypted websites to the temporary files. This slows down browsing for patrons who are logged into secure sites, but it will help to protect their privacy by never storing the files on the computer to begin with.

Firefox Settings

CONFIGURING FIREFOX

To access the history settings in Firefox, click on the Menu button, then click on History. This will open the history settings. You will see a window with all the recent history. From this window, you can choose the option to clear recent history.

Choosing this option brings up a small window that gives you the option to clear the history for the last hour, last two hours, last four hours, the day, or everything. You can be more specific about what type of history to clear by clicking on the Details button. This expands the window to show additional options. You can choose to clear the browsing and download history, forms and search history, cookies, cache, active logins, offline website data, and site prefer-ences. Browsing and download his-tory are comprised of the list of the

Firefox History

sites that were visited and when. Download history is the list of the files that were downloaded from sites; form history is the information that the user put into website forms; search history is a list of the terms that the user searched for on search engines; cookies are the cookies down-loaded from sites; the cache is the temporary files that were downloaded from sites.

When a user logs into a secure site, the browser can remember that login and restore it when the user, or any other user on the computer, opens that site again. Clearing active logins removes these remembered logins. Offline website data is information that sites store on the com-puter. Some sites store site information such as images and other data on the computer to make loading the site faster. Site preferences are settings that are set per site like zoom level, password restrictions, and pop-up blocker settings. Again, these preferences are saved as a con-venience to the user. However, when multiple individuals use the same computer, having this information available poses a privacy threat.

Firefox also has the ability to automatically clear history and cache files. You can find these options in the menu under Options.

1. In the options window, click on the Privacy option.

2. In the history section, click on the dropdown box next to "Firefox will:". You can select an option that tells the computer to remember history, never remember history, or use custom settings.

3. Choosing use custom settings opens additional options that allow you to specify how Firefox deals with search history.

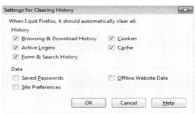

With Firefox, you can also choose to always use private browsing mode (discussed later in the chapter), and whether or not to remember brows-ing and download history, search

Firefox History Settings

and form history, and cookies. Unchecking an option stops Firefox from keeping that type of history. The cookies section allows you to set cookie preferences by site, what type of cookies to allow, and how long to keep cookies on the computer. Third-party cookies are cookies that are loaded on a site from a different site. For example, if you are visiting www.whateversite.com and that site wants to store a cookie from www.adsite.com on your computer, the cookie from www.adsite.com is considered a "third-party cookie."

You also have the option to automatically clear all history every time the browser is closed. Checking the box next to "clear history when Firefox closes," and then clicking on the Settings button opens the options to clear the history. The options are the same when clearing the history manually. You can clear the browsing and download history, active logins, form and search history, cookies, cache, saved passwords, site preferences, and offline website data.

Provide Safe Locations for Computers

Physical locations for public computers should also be a consideration for protecting the privacy of patrons. Since libraries are public buildings, it is difficult to create areas that grant patrons complete privacy. In some cases, providing too much physical privacy for a public computer creates a situation that patrons might use for activities that are not appropriate for public spaces. It is also often difficult for libraries to be able to provide a great deal of privacy for public computers due to lack of funds or lack of space.

The most common way to locate computers, and the most space efficient, is in rows as in a computer lab. Unfortunately, in this configuration, it is easy for people to view what is on the monitor of the person next to them. It is hard for patrons to hide what they are viewing on the computer from other computer users and passersby. In these situations, privacy screens on the monitor are an option to increase privacy. Many companies offer these flexible, tinted screens that are attached to the monitor. They are polarized and only allow light to pass through them at a particular angle—that is, when they are viewed straight on. If the person next to the monitor looks at the screen with the privacy filter on it, all they will see is a dark screen. Privacy filters are an easy way to give privacy in public areas; but they also are removable and can be stolen. Another drawback is that they tint the screen kind of like sunglasses do, and this can make it harder for patrons to see what is on the screen. Finally, they are also a little pricey. A standard privacy filter for a 19-inch-wide screen monitor can cost about $60.

Another option for building privacy is to create physical barriers. In a computer lab situation, dividers can be installed between computers. A divider like a short wall made of wood between the computer stations prevents people from being able to see what is on the monitor of their neighbor, and also allows each user to have their own private table space. Some companies make removable computer dividers, which means the area can be used for training. The downside of dividers is that although they are useful, they can also be very expensive. Installing them often means the library has to purchase either custom-built tables or new tables.

Individual computers not in labs can be situated in ways to provide a minimal amount of privacy. Turning tables so that they run along walls instead of against them grants a little security. Tables in open areas can be configured against each other, or in rows against each other to maximize the use of space, but still give a little privacy.

Privacy Audits

Some libraries conduct privacy audits of their systems to ensure that they are doing everything they can to protect their patrons' privacy. A privacy audit reviews all the systems at the library that relate to patron records and allows staff to find ways to protect that privacy. Since some privacy issues are a matter of state law, a privacy audit can also help to protect a library from potential legal issues.

A privacy audit should begin with a review of all library policies as they relate to patron privacy, both electronic records and paper records. Examples of policies that should be reviewed are a circulation policy that discusses handling of patron records, library record policies that cover storing patron checkout and usage records, and any policies related to overdue materials or collection agency accounts. Staff procedures regarding the creation of patron records like patron requests for interlibrary loans, computer usage, or technology checkouts for laptops or mobile devices should be reviewed. During these reviews, find ways to minimize the amount and type of information that is collected, what is done with the information after the transaction is complete, and how long the data is kept. For example, if you require patrons to fill out paper forms to request interlibrary loans or purchase requests, minimize the amount of information that is required by the user to fulfill the request. Sometimes forms are created that contain every piece of information about the requestor, but all that is really needed is just the name, phone number, and library card number. What information is needed is up to the library. Create a procedure to store the record only if it is needed beyond the transaction, and to destroy the record after the transaction is complete. If more than one staff member is involved in the transaction, review the storage of the records to make sure they are kept in a way that is protected against unauthorized users viewing them. If the requests are made in an electronic format on the library website, or by an outside vendor, make sure that the communication between the user and the online form is encrypted and is stored in a manner that is protected from outside intrusion. To ensure that the system is using a secure connection, contact the vendor or the hosting company for the library site and ask that the communication be encrypted. If the data is stored on your network, make sure the data is protected by a firewall and that the server itself is protected from unauthorized users. Servers should be stored in locations where they are physically protected from the public and from other staff members who do not need access to the server. If the data is stored on a vendor site, review the agreement or contract that the library has with the vendor to ensure that they are protecting the data from intrusion. Any agreements with third-party vendors should also be audited to review what the vendor does with the library data, how they dispose of it, and how they will deal with legal issues surrounding the library data.

When employees are hired, be sure they are given copies of all the library policies regarding privacy and security. Ask them to sign a form stating that they will abide by the state or local laws regarding confidentiality of library records and library policies.

Staff procedures regarding technology usage should be reviewed as well. Make sure staff understands that the library wishes to protect patrons' usage of technology. Staff should routinely follow any procedures to destroy paper records of usage and perform cleaning activities on computers such as rebooting computers or closing browsers.

Find ways to separate patron information from usage records. For some applications like patron materials requests or computer usage logs, the patron information can be purged from the record, but the usage of that resource can be retained.

Library Policies

Library policies should be reviewed to make sure that they are meeting the privacy needs of their users. Libraries have different policies related to privacy. Some of the most common policies are discussed here.

Library records policy—This policy is related to the records kept in relation to the use of the library including materials checked out. It frequently includes the types of records that are kept and how they are disposed of. It also should include information about how records are released, to whom, and under what conditions. For example: "Records related to a patron's checkout history will be turned over to the law enforcement agencies only in response to an order issued by a court of competent jurisdiction." This policy could be extended to include electronic records including public computer use. Add a statement like "Library records include any document, record, or other method of storing a record that identifies an individual's use of the library's services including interaction with staff, program attendance, or use of electronic services." It would be prudent to include a statement saying that the library attempts to protect the privacy of the user, but that it is impossible to guarantee the privacy of an individual on the Internet.

Website privacy policy—This policy is related to the web services that the library controls and provides to the patrons. It includes the type of information that the library collects when users use the library website, what is done with that data, and how it is stored and disposed of. The list of information that is collected when a user visits the site will change depending on the needs of the library, but typically includes:

- IP address of the visitor

- Browser type and version

- Operating system and version

- Date and time of the visit

- Pages that are viewed and for how long

- How they located the library website

The policy should specify what the information is used for. Once again, it will change depending on the needs of the library. For example:

- IP address—The IP address of the user visiting the library site is used to determine the location of the user and is purely for statistical purposes. It is also used to determine the number of visitors to the library site. No personally identifiable information is gathered or kept relating to the IP address.

- Browser type and version—The browser type and version for all visitors is collected and used to ensure that the services provided by the library are working for each type of browser and browser version.

- Operating system and version—The operating system and version are collected and used to ensure that the library web services are working for each type of operating system and version.

- Date and time of visit—The date and time of the visit to the library is stored for statistical use by the library.

- Pages that are viewed and for how long—The library wants to understand what parts of the website are being used and for how long. This information is gathered and used to determine what parts of the site are being used and what parts are not. It is also used for statistical information related to the number of pages viewed by visitors.

- How they located the site—The library stores how the site was located. For example, was a Google search used, or was a link from another site used? If an Internet search was used, the keywords used to find the site are also kept.

The policy should list how long the data is kept. For example:

> The library keeps this information in a database for a period of 1 year. This is to provide statistical data for the previous year. Beyond 1 year, only final figures are kept for long-term statistical evaluation, but the individual records are purged.

It is also useful to state what information the library is *not* collecting:

> The library does not store any personal information like name, address, credit card information, or any other type of personal information related to the use of the library website.

If the library uses the services of other companies for online services, like a credit card processor, or an online service like a book recommendation service or a database, that should be mentioned in the policy, and that the outside vendor has its own privacy policies. It should specify the sites where the policy is valid. For example:

> This policy covers the privacy of the following sites:
>
> - www.mylibrary.com
> - catalog.mylibrary.com
> - www.mylibrarydatabases.com
>
> The library uses other sites for the purposes of donations and fee payments, online databases, and other services. The policy does not extend to those sites. Once a visitor leaves the sites listed above, the privacy policies of those sites takes effect. For any questions related to the privacy of personal information on other sites, contact the operators of those sites.

The policy should also state that if patrons provide the library with any personally identifiable information, they are providing it willingly, and it should explain what the library will do with that information. For example:

> Any personally identifying information provided by a visitor to the library website is provided willingly by the visitor. The information collected may include:
>
> - Name
> - Address
> - Phone number
> - Email account
>
> This information is given to the library for the purposes of feedback to the library's online services, questions about the library or its services, and registration for library services. If this information is provided, it is stored in a database in relation to the purpose and is only used for the intended purpose of the visitor. The library will never use the information for any other purpose, sell it, or give it to any other party for any reason.

Internet use policy—This policy is frequently in place at libraries to specify what types of online services are provided by the library, and how the patrons are expected to use them. It usually has sections on "acceptable use." For example:

- Patrons must not use the Internet to intend harm on other users, or on library systems (no viruses or malware).

- Patrons must not use the Internet for spam.

- Patrons must not use the Internet to access illegal information such as child pornography or stealing copyrighted materials such as movies or music.

Usually the policy has a section on Internet safety. For example:

> The Internet is a large resource that includes useful information and services and activities for many people. It should not be considered a safe place. It is possible for anyone using the Internet to have their privacy stolen. The library attempts to put in place measures to protect the privacy and safety of library users on the Internet, but it is not possible to guarantee that safety. The Internet is also a source of misinformation, and users of the Internet should exercise judgment and evaluate for themselves the value of any information accessed online. The library does not guarantee that all the information accessed online is true and accurate.

The policy should have information about personal devices used on the library networks. For example:

> Any device that is not the property of the library is allowed to connect to the library systems using the public wireless access point. The wireless network is called LibraryFreePublicWiFi. Any user connecting their personal devices to this network must comply with all applicable sections of this policy. Any device shown to be engaging in any activity that is illegal, or is detrimental to the operation of the wi-fi network, will be removed from the service and could be banned from connecting again.

Library policies are an important aspect of public services and need to be carefully written. Before instituting any policy in the library, especially related to Internet use, it is advisable to review policies of other libraries, or to seek the help of other libraries. In some situations, it might be required to have policies reviewed by legal counsel before they are put in place.

Policies set the way a library operates and have a lot of control over the level of privacy that a library can attempt to give to the patrons. They also protect the library with expectations for the way patrons use the library services. Changing staff procedures can provide a high level of protection for library users. Clearing usage logs from reservation systems and network devices can clear saved histories of computer usage. Configuring browsers to automatically clear patron usage protects library users on public computers.

Bibliography

American Library Association. "Public Library Funding & Technology Access Study 2011–2012." http://www.ala.org/research/plftas/2011_2012

Illinois Library Association. "Protecting Library Patron Confidentiality—Checklist of Best Practices." Last updated fall 2006, http://www.ila.org/advocacy-files/pdf/Confidentiality_Best_Practices.pdf

Privacy Rights Clearinghouse. "Online Privacy: Using the Internet Safely." Last updated October 2014, https://www.privacyrights.org/online-privacy-using-internet-safely

CHAPTER 3

Patron Education

Patron Education

Libraries have a long history of providing assistance to patrons on using technology. According to a recent study on public computers, 98 percent of public libraries provided some type of training for their patrons on using technology (Information Policy & Access Center, 2014). Libraries that provide technology assistance to their patrons offer classes on how to use library resources, general Internet usage, general computer and software skills, and safe online practices. However, while the percentage of libraries offering classes on library skills and Internet, computer, and software skills is in the 90 percent range, only around 60 percent of libraries offer patrons classes on safe practices on the Internet (Information Policy & Access Center, 2014). This author asserts that along with the standard classes, libraries should provide sessions for patrons on threats to privacy on the Internet, and how they can keep themselves safe on the Internet. After all, teaching patrons how to use the Internet, but not how to use it safely is like showing someone how to drive a car, but not where the seatbelt is.

Classes on Internet privacy need not be overly comprehensive or cover every aspect of how to protect privacy. It is not necessary for all patrons, especially those learning the basics of the Internet, to be given a full understanding of Internet security. A basic understanding of how the Internet works and some simple ways that patrons can increase their safety would be sufficient for most cases. You can integrate this topic into any existing classes that cover usage of the Internet. Consider introducing the idea of Internet security and privacy in beginning Internet skills classes, while covering the topic in more depth in your more advanced Internet skills classes. All other types of educational classes that use the Internet can add basic security skills as well. For example, a class on how to sell items on eBay could discuss password safety, while a class on how to edit photographs online could discuss basic browser security.

Some ideas for classes for patrons include the following:

- **Browsing the Internet safely**—In this class, cover topics on how to create accounts safely, and how to log into them using extra layers of security. Password safety should be emphasized, and how to browse the Internet using secure connections. Two versions of this class could be offered, one for teens and younger adults, and one for senior citizens.

- **Configuring your browser to protect your privacy**—This class aimed at more advanced users could cover how to automatically clear the browser history, how to use private mode browsing, and what types of browser plug-ins (covered in chapter 6) can be installed to protect privacy.

- **Personal computer safety**—This class should cover the basics of browsing the Web safely, as well as how to configure the browser, and include information on how users can protect their own computer. This includes how to install and maintain an antivirus application, and how to install applications to clean personal information from the computer.

- **Anonymous Internet use**—This class could really dig into the topic of private Internet browsing and show how to use proxies and Tor (covered in chapter 5). It should also discuss the same information as the classes on configuring your browser and browsing the Internet safely.

Other classes could be built depending on the needs of the library and its patrons. For example, a kids' class could be put together that shows how to be safe on the Internet.

The following sections discuss the possible topics for patron education classes. They include ways that patrons can be more secure and safe using the Internet, how to create accounts on online sites, how to protect their computer, and ways to search the Internet more privately.

Password Security

Using the Internet today requires us to manage passwords. Be sure to give your patrons, especially those who are learning to use the Internet for the first time, the basic ideas behind password security. Explain that if their account is compromised, it becomes accessible to others who can use the patron's information. Depending on the type of account being compromised, the hacker could send out spam messages from the account, steal the victim's identity, get financial information, and even hack into the user's bank account to steal money.

There are common strategies that people use to create safer passwords. Word or letter substitution, uppercase characters, special characters, and length are all ways to improve password security.

- **Avoid using common words or phrases**—Many people use something very identifiable as their password like their last name or street address. Anyone who knows even the smallest amount of information about a person can easily guess those passwords. When choosing a password, pick either nonsense words, or words that have no relation to you in any way.

- **Word or letter substitution**—This is changing a word or a character in the password to something else. This helps to keep a password easier to remember, but harder to guess. For example, you could take the password spooky46 and substitute the oo in spooky with the number 0. Now the password looks like this: sp00ky46. It is still easy to remember that password, but it is more difficult to guess it since it strays from the dictionary spelling. Word substitution is taking the words in the password and replacing them with something else. It could be as simple as taking the words "I Love My Library," taking the first letter of each word, ILML, and using that as a password. Now the user password is as easy as remembering the phrase "I Love My Library." These days, passwords are increasingly becoming case sensitive. That means the passwords LibrariesRock and librariesrock are two completely different passwords due to the uppercase letters in the first one. This makes it easier to create a secure password by simply adding uppercase letters throughout the password. For example, the password library1234 is pretty easy to guess, but if you add a few uppercase letters randomly in it—liBrAry1234—it becomes a little more difficult to guess.

- **Use special characters**—Some sites allow special characters to be used in a password, which is another way of increasing security. Special characters are any nonalphanumeric characters on the keyboard. The alphanumeric keys are all the letters and numbers. Special characters would include the exclamation mark, question mark, parenthesis, percent sign, and so on. These can be used as letter substitutions like Libr&ary233, or just inserted into passwords to make them more difficult: lib!@rary(1).

- **Make long passwords**—Passwords should be as long as possible to reduce the likelihood of being guessed. An average password should be at least 8–10 characters long, but longer if possible.

- **Use different passwords**—This one is difficult for many people. It is easy to create a nice, strong password, then use it everywhere. If a password is compromised in one place from a hack or some other type of attack, then the person who gained access to the password also has access to all the other accounts for the same person.

- **Change them frequently**—This is another difficult one for many people. Once a good password is created, people resist changing it. Passwords should be changed as frequently as possible, but within reason. For most accounts, passwords should be changed as often as possible without creating problems. If a password is changed too frequently, the likelihood of it being forgotten is much higher. Most sites that require password changes suggest changing them every 3–6 months. Many sites offer recovery questions or other methods to recover a lost password. These should be set so that if a password is forgotten, it is easier to recover it. When setting these recovery questions, try not to use very common questions like "What street do you live on?" or "What is your spouse's name?" If you can create your own recovery questions, try to make them as obscure as possible, something that no one else would know the answer to. Some sites like Google or Facebook offer the ability to send a text message to your phone to recover a lost password.

Using a combination of these password techniques should create a password that is difficult to guess or hack, but yet is still somewhat easy to remember.

Secure Browsing

Patrons need to understand that information being transmitted over the Internet is, most of the time, being sent in a manner that can be intercepted and read by a third party. If they are performing a transaction over the Internet that requires an extra level of security like a financial transaction or a personal bank or stock transaction, they should make sure that their browser is in a secure mode.

Secure Page

The simplest way to confirm that is to locate the URL in the address bar and make sure it has HTTPS at the beginning. The S in the location stands for secure. This means that the browser has negotiated a secure transaction with the remote browser, and the communication between them is almost impossible to decipher. Most browsers also show a lock somewhere to show that the secure transaction has been started. Bogus sites or sites that try to steal a patron's information may show all kinds of icons or statements that they are secure, but without the HTTPS or the lock icon in the browser, the communication is not secure.

Account Settings

Almost every site we use on the Internet wants us to create an account. Often sites require users to have an account in order to view information, order something, or use their services. When creating online accounts, it is important to understand the dangers involved in the personal information given out. Many sites ask their visitors to provide them with many personal details. This can be during a simple registration or to complete some kind of transaction. Some sites use this information to provide a better experience for the visitor, or to tailor their site to make it more useful. However, although this may be useful, the site can also use the personal information for other purposes. For example, many sites sell user information to advertisers or use the information to market their products more efficiently to the visitor. Most sites provide a privacy policy that is readily available and details what information the site collects, how they use it, and what they can do with it. When teaching or coaching patrons about Internet safety, show patrons examples of privacy policies and where they are located on the average site. Make sure they understand that during registration or transactions, not all information is required. Sites show required fields with a red asterisk or some other type of visual clue. Many sites also offer users the option to complete certain transactions or view certain materials without having to have an account. Look for the option to check out as a guest or to continue as a guest.

For sites that do require an account to use their services, take some time to view the account settings and look for opportunities to opt out of certain transactions. Most sites offer you the choice to opt out of email communications or to not contact the user for any reason. More complicated account settings, like the settings at Google, also allow the user to opt out of targeted advertising.

For Google, these settings are located in the Account Settings section.

- Go to www.google.com and click on Sign In at the upper left.
- Once logged in, click on your account picture, then go to Account. On the Account page, you should see Account History at the top.

Google Sign In Page. Google and the Google logo are registered trademarks of Google Inc., used with permission.

- Clicking on the Account History option shows a list of Google products, and near the bottom under Related Settings is Ads.

- Click on Edit Settings next to Ads. This page allows you to manage how Google treats you in regard to advertising. While you're browsing the Web, any sites

Google Ad Settings. Google and the Google logo are registered trademarks of Google Inc., used with permission.

that are owned by Google or have ads placed on them by Google ad services will take into account your settings on this page. You can provide or remove any information that you do not wish Google to know. You can even give Google incorrect information. Near the bottom of the page there is the option to opt out of interest-based ads on Google sites and sites that use Google ads. Opting out of interest-based ads disables all the settings on this page.

Account Logins on Public Computers

It is also important to stress the importance of managing account logins on public computers. Often patrons log into their personal accounts on public computers; when they are done, they just close the browser and walk away. Unless the library has configured the computers to clear the browser history or restore it to a clean state, the next person who opens the browser and opens a page that the previous user was using can see all the previous person's information including the sites the user visited, what pages they viewed on the sites, and potentially their personal information like email, bank account information, or any other site that the previous user logged into, but did not log out of. This can happen easily with email accounts where the login is kept as a persistent login. With a persistent login, the login information is stored in a secure cookie, so the next time the browser is opened and that site is accessed, it will open the previous account.

The Google login page displays the option to "stay signed in," which is checked by default. When you log in to Google and leave this box checked, your account login remains, even if the browser is closed. This functionality is great for a personal computer or a work computer where you and only you log in regularly; but at a public computer, for example in a library, leaving a single user's login on the computer poses a threat. Be sure this box is always unchecked and inform users to always log out of their accounts before they close the browser.

With online services such as Outlook email and Facebook, this option is unchecked by default, so the user does not remained logged in once the browser is closed; but with other services such as Google, Yahoo, and Twitter the "signed in" option is the default. So, it's important to check with each service to make sure your information is not made accessible to others using the computer.

One of the most often hacked accounts for individuals is email accounts. Hackers wish to gain access to a user's email account so they can use a verified, functional email account to send spam out or to send email to the user's address book. Once a spammer gains access to an email account, they will use it as a gateway to send out spam all over the world. Usually, the email provider picks up on this pretty quickly and closes the account; but even if it can be used for a day or two, the account is useful, allowing hundreds of thousands of spam emails to be sent out.

Hackers also use a compromised account to send email to the victim's address book. The message they send is usually something along the lines of "I was traveling and lost my wallet and cannot pay for a hotel or food, etc." They then make a plea for their friends and family to send them money. Since the message comes from a trusted friend or family member, it is more likely to get a response. Compromised email accounts also give up all the personal information about the victim to the hacker. This information could include anything that the user has put into their profile including their name, phone number, address, and so on. It would also include any information in emails the user sent or received. This could be very personal information including addresses, Social Security number, age, name, address, and the like. The hacker can then use this information to steal the identity of the victim—withdraw money from bank accounts, open new credit cards under the victim's name, make charges to those credit cards, and so forth. To help protect against these kinds of attacks, several email providers have created additional authentication methods. Google, for example, has a two-step verification method that users can use to make sure their account is not compromised. In a two-step verification authentication, when the user logs into their account with their username and password, they must authenticate again using a different method that is more secure and unlikely to be compromised. In the case of Google, the two-step verification uses a PIN code that is sent to a mobile phone number that must be entered before the account can be accessed.

To set up the two-step verification in Google:

- Go to www.google.com and log into your account.

- Go to your account settings by clicking on your account picture at the upper right side and clicking on Account.

- At the top of the page, click on Security, then Setup next to the two-step verification.

Google Two-Step Verification. Google and the Google logo are registered trademarks of Google Inc., used with permission.

- Click on the Start Setup button and choose the contact phone number and method. Google supports both a voice call and a text message that can be sent to a mobile number. Using the voice method is the only option for work phones or other phones that do not accept text messages. When you click on the Send Code button, Google sends a code to the mobile phone specified that you must type into the next box. This verifies that you have access to the phone you specified, and that you did not make any mistakes when typing in the phone number.

- After verifying the phone, you can choose to trust the computer you are on. This is useful for a personal computer or a work computer that you access all the time and do not need two-step verification on. You can add or delete trusted computers in the account settings. The trusted computer setting is also used to gain access to your account should your phone be lost or stolen.

Two-Step Login Code Page. Google and the Google logo are registered trademarks of Google Inc., used with permission.

Now that two-step verification is turned on, whenever you attempt to log into your account, you are prompted to enter the verification code that is sent to the mobile phone specified in the account.

Google also offers several backup options you can use to gain access to your account using the two-step verification process, which is handy if your phone is unavailable, lost, or if you are in a place that does not have cell service. You can print out a list of one-time codes that grants you emergency access to your account. Google suggests you print out the codes and put them in a wallet or purse. If you were traveling and needed to access your account, but you lost your cell phone, normal two-step verification would not work. With a list of one-time codes, you can use one of them to access your account instead of the text message. You would still need your regular password to access the account. The codes are useless without them. You can also add additional phones to the verification list. Using this, you could add a family member's phone or a work phone. This is useful in the event your phone is lost or damaged and you need to gain access to your account. A second phone provides a backup to the first phone.

Keep in mind that if you turn on two-step verification for your email services, you will have to reauthenticate any devices or services that access that account. For example, if you use Gmail on your mobile phone, after you turn on two-step verification, the Gmail client on your mobile phone will stop working until you reauthenticate to the client using the new two-step authentication.

Other services offer similar two-step verification. Facebook has a security service called Login Approvals. When you attempt to log into Facebook using a computer that has not been identified as a safe browser, the system sends you a verification

Facebook Login Approvals

code using the Facebook mobile app installed on a mobile device like an Android phone, iPhone, or iPad. To use this service:

- Log into your Facebook account, go to the Account Settings, then to the Security Settings page.
- Check the box next to the Login Approvals option and click Save Changes. The system will ask you what type of device you are using. After choosing the device type, you must log into the Facebook mobile app on the device you are using.
- Click on the Menu option, then touch Code Generator and Activate. The app will generate a code. Type that code into the webpage for confirmation.

Now when you log into Facebook from a computer that is not recognized as trusted, Facebook will ask you to generate a code on the mobile app to verify your login. You can also add a mobile phone number to the login approval process, so the system will send a text instead of using the mobile app.

Many other online services offer a form of two-step verification. Some of the most common sites that offer this are Twitter, LinkedIn, Dropbox, Microsoft, Yahoo Mail, and Apple.

Some common sites do not offer two-step verification for logins. Some of these are Amazon, AOL, Mail.com, Instagram, Netflix, and Hulu. Many financial institutions do not support two-step authentication, including TurboTax, Quickbooks Online, Sharebuilder, Scottrade, Square, Capital One, Citibank, and Wells Fargo.

For a list of sites that support or that do not support two-step authentication, see https://twofactorauth.org/.

Location Verification

Several email providers including Outlook, Google, and Yahoo also have a location verification system that allows users to see the last time and location that their account was accessed. If someone else gains unauthorized access to your email account, you would be aware of it due to an odd location in the login history for the account. In Google, the account activity is located at the bottom of the mail page. It shows the last time the account was active and where else the account is logged in. If you click on the Details option, it shows a full list of the locations and times that the account was accessed. By looking at the list you can quickly locate any odd or unknown logins. If a strange login is detected, you should change your password immediately.

Last account activity: 2 minutes ago
Open in 1 other location Details

Google Location Verification. Google and the Google logo are registered trademarks of Google Inc., used with permission.

Location Verification Details. Google and the Google logo are registered trademarks of Google Inc., used with permission.

You can also create an alert for any strange logins by clicking on the option at the bottom of the page. With this option turned on, you will receive alert emails from Google when the system detects strange logins from a variety of locations.

Antivirus Applications

When coaching or teaching patrons about the Internet, always stress that they should use antivirus applications on their personal computers. As discussed in chapter 1, some viruses and spyware applications are designed to steal the private information of the user on an infected computer. Most computers come with some kind of antivirus application installed when they are purchased. However, these preinstalled applications are usually trial applications that expire after 90 days or a year. These preinstalled applications will notify users when they have expired. This is usually a message that appears when they log into the computer. If users are unsure if they have a preinstalled antivirus application, they can look through the information that came with the computer when they purchased it, or look in the control panel to see if one is installed. To check this,

1. On Windows 7, click on the Start button, then on Control Panel.
2. Click on the option to uninstall a program. This will open up a new window with a list of all the programs on the computer.
3. On Windows 8, go to the start screen and click on the down arrow at the bottom of the screen to see all the apps.
4. In the Windows System section, click on the Control Panel.
5. From the Control Panel, click on the option to Uninstall a Program.

From the list of applications that are installed on the computer, look for the antivirus application that was preinstalled on the computer. There are many possible applications, but the most popular are Norton Antivirus and McAfee. If they have a preinstalled application that has expired, patrons should either renew the subscription for the preinstalled application or purchase a new antivirus application. Some free applications are discussed in chapter 4.

Before purchasing or even relying on an antivirus application, users should verify that the antivirus application protects against viruses and spyware. Most of the popular applications available have support for both viruses and spyware applications. The most popular antivirus applications available are the following:

- **Bitdefender**—This is a paid application that excelled on many comparison charts. It protects against viruses and spyware and has some online protection including a pop-up blocker. It is available at http://www.bitdefender.com/.

- **AVG Antivirus**—This is a free antivirus application. Even though it is free, it still ranks high on many reviews. It protects against viruses and spyware, and includes a "Do Not Track" feature that attempts to identify sites that are tracking the user's information and offers the ability to block it. There is more information about AVG in chapter 5. It is available at http://free.avg.com/us-en/free-antivirus-download.

- **AVAST! Antivirus**—This is another free application that rates well. It blocks viruses and spyware. It is available at http://www.avast.com/en-us/index.

- **Norton Antivirus**—Norton is one of the largest antivirus applications. It is a paid application and frequently comes preinstalled on new computers. It rates pretty well on some comparison lists. It protects against viruses and spyware, and comes with alerts for sites it considers dangerous and an identity safe with a password to help protect online identities. It is available at http://us.norton.com/.

Search Behavior

As discussed in chapter 1, search engines keep records of all searches performed by users. They log the IP address of the search and what search terms were used. They sometimes also store the location of the search request. In the case of some search engines, like Google, the search history is specifically stored for the logged-in user account. This is useful for individuals who want to remember what terms they previously used to search for a particular piece of information or a specific site. Google can also suggest further research on topics the user searched for.

However, just as other stored information can pose a danger to users, this function can also work against them. Be sure your patrons understand how to view and disable this feature, or how to choose different search engines, such as StartPage and DuckDuckGo, mentioned later in this chapter, that do not track their behavior.

In Google, you must log into the account first to view or change the search history. To do this, go to www.google.com and log into the account. Click on the Settings option, then on History. This brings up a page with all the search history for the user. On the left side you can view the history for the different products that Google offers including the Web, news, shopping, books, maps, and so on. Next to each search term, you can check the box, and then choose Remove items from the top of the list. This removes them from the history. To remove all the items from the history, click on the settings gear at the upper right and choose Remove items. From the box that appears, choose from the beginning of time, or any time period you want. After that, click on the Remove button to perform the removal.

Google Search History. Google and the Google logo are registered trademarks of Google Inc., used with permission.

You can also simply disable the Search History option. This prevents Google from storing the search history in the first place. To do this:

1. Go to the main Google page again, www.google.com, and login.

2. Click on the Settings option at the lower right and then on Search Settings.

3. From this page, near the bottom, click on the option for Search History.

4. From the Search History page, click on the settings gear, then on Settings.

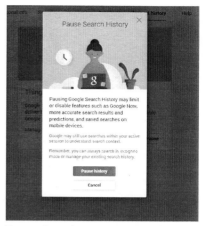

Pause Search History. Google and the Google logo are registered trademarks of Google Inc., used with permission.

5. On this page, click on the button that says Pause next to the Manage History option. This brings up a box telling you that some Google features and products may not work as well with the search history turned off. There are several Google products that use the search history to provide better information to the user. For example, the Google Now product available on mobile devices uses the search history to recommend Internet sites, products, and nearby events to the user. With the search history turned off, Google will still work, but it will not be able to personalize its features based on Internet searches. Also, if the search history is turned off, users will not be able to view their search history on different devices. If you want to turn it off, click on the Pause History button. Until you enable the search history again on this page, Google will no longer keep it. Turning off the search history turns it off for all devices that the person uses. If someone has a mobile phone or a tablet device with Google services on it, this will disable them as well.

Using a different search engine is another possibility for patrons who want to be able to use the Internet without having their searches recorded. There are several search engines that provide confidential searching abilities. Two of the top ones are StartPage and DuckDuckGo.

StartPage

You can find StartPage at www.startpage.com. The benefit of Start-Page is that any searches performed with their search engine are

stripped of any identifying information and then submitted to Google. The search results are returned to you through their interface so Google is not aware of who performed the search. StartPage also defaults to a secure connection, so any searches performed on the site are encrypted and protected.

StartPage Search Engine

DuckDuckGo

DuckDuckGo is another search engine that provides private searches. They do not store any information about the searches performed, nor do

DuckDuckGo

they store any identifiable information about the user, IP address, web browser, and so forth.

DuckDuckGo aggregates search data from multiple sources and returns them to the user. For regular searches, DuckDuckGo will use crowdsourcing sites like Wikipedia directly, or other search engines like Yandex, Yahoo, Bing, and Wolfram Alpha.

DuckDuckGo Search Engine

Other Search Engines

Other search engines that offer privacy features are:

- **Ixquick** (www.ixquick.com)—Ixquick is from the same company that offers StartPage. The difference between the two is that Ixquick aggregates search results from other search engines including Google. It offers the same privacy features as StartPage.

- **Blekko** (www.blekko.com)—Blekko does not offer complete privacy searching like DuckDuckGo or StartPage. It logs personally identifying information, but deletes it after 48 hours. If you create an account with Blekko, you can disable data collection entirely.

Educating patrons on how to use the Internet more securely and providing them with a better understanding of how privacy works on the Internet and how they can browse more privately is valuable for the patrons and for the library. Libraries are sources of information. Everyone needs to know how to use the Internet to find information with accuracy and safety, and not have to worry about the loss of their privacy.

Bibliography

Information Policy & Access Center. "Public Libraries and the Internet." Last Updated 2014, http://www.plinternetsurvey.org/analysis/public-libraries-and -community-access

CHAPTER 4

Network Security and Devices

Network Security and Devices

Network Design

Most libraries connect their public devices to the Internet using a network. Networks are a way to connect devices together in order to share resources like printers, servers, software, and Internet connections. To create a network, the IT specialists connect devices together using a variety of specialized hardware like switches, routers, and firewalls, some of which can be configured to assist in protecting the individual privacy of the user as well as the security of the devices.

To get started with changes to the network or the devices on the network, it is important to discuss the changes with a network specialist who can assist you in making the changes. Networks are complicated, and even small changes can affect the overall performance and security of the entire network. Finding the right mix of safety and security for the users on the network and providing a stable, high-performance network is difficult.

This chapter does not cover all the devices that are on a network. It is possible that additional devices may be on the network that can assist in providing additional layers of privacy and security for the users. Once again, discuss these ideas with a network specialist who can help.

Routers

When a computer or other device connects to the Internet, its communication is sent through a router. Routers are basic building blocks of computer networks, used to translate communication between two different networks. In this case, the two networks are the library computer network and the Internet. As traffic passes through the router, the router translates the communication and creates log entries of that traffic. These logs contain the

- IP address of the computer
- Destination site on the Internet
- Date and time of the communication

These logs are very useful to network technicians who monitor the usage of the networks, manage the network traffic, and diagnose issues or problems with the network or the router. Since the logs also show what computer went where on the Internet and when, they can also be used to determine what sites a particular user visited during their use of the device. It may not be possible to fully determine what user went where, since a patron using a public computer in a library may not have their identity tied to a particular computer at a particular time, but if the library also keeps logs of computer usage by patrons, it is possible.

Routers also have another basic feature that can be useful in creating a level of anonymity while on the Internet. Every device on the Internet is assigned a unique identifier called an Internet Protocol address or IP address. When devices connect to and communicate with Internet servers, the connection is made with the IP address. The Internet server that is communicating creates logs of the IP addresses that request information from it. These logs can be used to determine which computer was communicating with the server at a specific time.

IP addresses are allocated by an organization called the Internet Assigned Numbers Authority. IP addresses are granted to any organization that wishes to have access directly to the Internet. Since the cost of creating and maintaining an Internet connection and purchasing IP addresses can be quite high, most libraries purchase their access, and thus their IP address, from a local Internet provider. Many networks in libraries are very large, with hundreds or more Internet-capable devices on them. It is not practical for the library to have a unique IP address for each device on their network, since that would require the purchase of more IP addresses from their Internet provider. Instead, the network makes use of a technology in routers called Network Address Translation or NAT.

NAT basically takes one address or addresses and makes them look like another single address. In this situation, a network can have 100 different computers, each with its own unique, private address. Using NAT, they translate all their private addresses into a single public IP address. With this system, any device on a private network with a private address appears to a remote Internet server as the single public IP address the library has purchased.

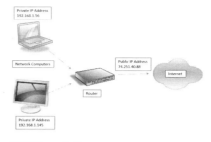

NAT Translation

While using NAT, all individual computers on a library network appear to be the same device on the Internet, but only when taking into account their IP address. As discussed before, devices still broadcast other information about themselves, and communication between two devices can provide even more information. Although using NAT is not the most effective way to provide privacy to individual computers, it still provides a simple, basic way to mask a computer's IP from any kind of Internet spying that relies on IP for tracking.

Configuring NAT

Most routers use NAT or are configured for NAT by default. Configuration in this case would be as simple as connecting more than one device to the router using either the onboard Ethernet ports or connecting a switch to the router. Switches take one Ethernet computer port and expand it to more ports. When devices are connected to the switch, they are given an IP address by the router that will use NAT to route their traffic to the Internet. For more detailed instructions on how to configure NAT, refer to the documentation or support materials for the router you use.

Subnetting

Good network design includes the creation of what are called "subnets" to segregate the network into logical segments. When devices are connected to a network, they are given IP addresses that allow them to communicate with devices on the network, including printers and servers, and to give them a route to the Internet. When a network administrator creates the network that the devices connect to, they assign a range of IP addresses that those devices can use. When a network grows too large, or if there is a need to create logical separation between devices, an administrator can create two or more groups of IP addresses and put devices into one of them based on the need. There are many reasons to create separate subnets. Many public libraries create a subnet for staff computers and devices, another for public computers and devices, and a third for wireless users and devices. When devices are subnetted from each other, they cannot see each other or interact unless an administrator has created rules on the router or firewall to allow the communication. This allows the administrator to protect the staff computers from the public computers, which are more likely to become infected with viruses or malware, or to be used by patrons to attempt to hack into the library computers. Subnetting also allows an administrator to separate and allocate devices that only certain groups of computers are allowed to use. When used in conjunction with a firewall, a subnet can also create and enforce rules to protect privacy.

Creation of a subnet is not a difficult process, but there are too many devices and possibilities to consider when creating a subnetted network. For more information on how to configure a subnet for your network, contact the manufacturer of your firewall or router.

Firewalls

A firewall is a barrier between devices to separate networks. In most cases, a firewall protects the devices on the private side of the firewall from devices on the public side of the firewall. Rules are used on the firewall to specify what communication is allowed between the two sides of the firewall. Firewalls protect networks from malicious attacks coming from the Internet, viruses getting onto or off private computers, spyware grabbing personal information off computers, and more. They can also be used to block unwanted communication, including activities that take away a user's privacy.

Most computers come with a software version of a firewall. Since the release of Windows XP, Microsoft Windows has included a small firewall to protect the individual computer. Many antivirus applications like Norton or McAfee also include a software firewall that provides limited protection from the Internet; but in most cases, a software firewall is very limited in the types of communication it can protect against, and a hardware firewall is highly recommended for networks. Software firewalls often are not intelligent enough to truly understand the type of communication that is passing through them. They are mainly designed to block a particular type of communication. For example, many applications want to connect to the Internet to update themselves, like Java. When the Java application makes an attempt to connect to the Internet to check for updates, the software firewall on the computer will see this attempt and ask the user if they want to allow it. The software firewall is not determining what the communication is; it is just allowing it or disallowing it. A more complicated hardware firewall would be able to analyze the actual communication passing through and make a decision on whether to allow it or not. For example, a virus may use an existing connection to transmit to the Internet. A hardware firewall would be more likely to catch this transmission.

In this example, all the computers on the network are attached to the firewall, and the Internet router is attached to the other side of the firewall. Configuring the network in this manner assures that all the Internet communication going to or from this network must go through the firewall.

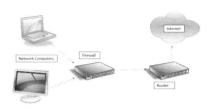

Network with a Firewall

How Does a Firewall Protect Privacy?

Since a firewall is constantly watching all the traffic that passes through it, it is able to filter the traffic. IT administrators can create rules for firewalls that allow or deny certain types of communication. Usually, these rules are created to prevent an attacker from gaining access to the devices on the network. Many viruses communicate in ways that can be identified by a firewall. For example, most viruses, when they infect a computer, will attempt to send copies of themselves to other computers. A common method is to create email connections and email other people copies of itself. A firewall can see an infected computer attempting to make a large number of email connections on the Internet and block that communication from happening. Once a firewall identifies a certain communication as being a virus, it can block it. Spyware applications also have identifiable communication that firewalls can identify. Many spyware applications will want to connect to servers on the Internet to send out information about the user, or to attempt to install on other computers. The firewall can see an infected computer attempting to connect to known spyware servers on the Internet and block that communication.

Newer firewalls automatically have lists that can be subscribed to. These lists identify specific spyware applications, viruses, advertising sites, and other types of malware. If your library subscribes to one or more of these lists, you can use them to create exclusions in the firewall and prevent harmful communications from getting to the public computers.

For example, Sonicwall firewalls have an advanced subscription for spyware applications. With this feature turned on, the firewall inspects all incoming and outgoing traffic to determine if it fits within the antispyware rules. If it does, the firewall can block the communication, or allow it and log it.

Sonicwall Firewall Application Settings

Wireless Access Points

A wireless access point allows wireless clients to connect to a network. Any library that offers wireless access for their patrons has a wireless access point somewhere in the building. Often, the wireless access point is part of the router that came from the Internet provider and is configured through that device.

When wireless clients connect to the access point, they are given an IP address either by the wireless access point or by the router on the network. Depending on the configuration of the network, this could mean that the devices connected to the same network as the wireless clients might be able to see each other.

The best solution for keeping wireless access points safe is to have them configured to be on their own subnet. That way, all the wireless clients are separated from the library staff computers and the regular public computers on the network. You can configure the subnet on the wireless access point, or you can create a subnet on the network using a switch and then connect that wireless access point to that subnet.

It is worth noting that wireless clients on a wireless network are able to "see" each other. This is due to the way the network is created. Each device on the wireless network is given an IP address that is part of the same set of addresses as the other devices. It is possible for someone to scan the list of IP addresses on the wireless network and then attempt to connect to devices that respond to a scan. Depending on the configuration of the computer that is being scanned, it is possible that the computer could respond to other devices. Newer versions of Windows have a media-sharing feature that could allow other people on a wireless network to see the media on other computers. This allows for sharing of resources. For example, if there were a printer on the network with the wireless clients, those clients could search the network, see the printer, connect to it, and use it. This also goes for media applications. Windows allows users to share their media, music, videos, and pictures to devices on a network. If this service is turned on for a wireless client, then it is possible for other clients on the same wireless network to "see" each other—and share the same resources, media, and so on. It is also possible for some types of viruses and spyware applications to use networks to find clients to attack. For these reasons, wireless access points offer a feature called wireless isolation. With wireless isolation, the wireless access point hides the clients from each other. They are not able to see each other, so it appears to the clients as if they are on the network alone. Wireless isolation is supported by most wireless access point manufacturers.

To enable wireless isolation, connect to the administrative interface for your wireless access point or router. The setting is usually located on the wireless page or under advanced settings. For Linksys routers, it is located on the Advanced Wireless Settings page under Wireless. Netgear routers have the option under the Wireless settings. If you cannot locate the setting, contact the manufacturer for your access point or router.

Networks are useful and offer many different ways to protect the users on them. Networks are designed to share resources and to promote communication between the devices on the network and the remote networks, like the Internet they connect to. Managing the way the devices can communicate with each other with routers and providing layers of protection with firewalls can offer additional safety and security for the users. Privacy will also be increased when providing these additional safety and security measures.

Bibliography

Howstuffworks. "How Network Address Translation Works." Accessed December 20, 2014, http://computer.howstuffworks.com/nat.htm

How-To-Geek. "Lock Down Your Wi-Fi Network with Your Router's Wireless Isolation Option." Accessed December 20, 2014, http://www.howtogeek.com/179089/lock-down-your-wi-fi-network-with-your-routers-wireless-isolation-option/

TechRepublic. "IP Subnetting Made Easy." Last modified March 3, 2009, http://www.techrepublic.com/blog/data-center/ip-subnetting-made-easy-125343/

CHAPTER 5

Windows Settings and Applications

Windows Settings and Applications

Public computers that are running on the Windows operating system can be configured to provide some level of protection for the individuals using them. First of all, the Windows operating system has several built-in features that can be configured to prevent user data from being saved or sent out over the Internet. Windows also has policies that can be configured to create a more secure environment and to help delete private data. In addition, there are some applications that can be installed on the computer to help clear data or prevent it from staying on the computer. Internet browsers can be configured with add-ons or extensions that help to protect a user's privacy on the Internet.

Windows Policies

(Please note that parts of this section on Windows policies assumes that you already have a Windows Active Domain installed and configured and that Group Policies are turned on. Providing instructions for the installation and configuration of an Active Domain is beyond the scope of this book.)

Microsoft Windows offers a set of policies that can be used to modify the behavior of the operating system or the applications installed on the computer. These policies can be used to modify almost any behavior of the computer including user and system security, behavior of the operating system, and how applications behave. They can be used to control the settings of Internet Explorer. Settings can be forced on the application, and the ability to change them or delete them can be removed.

In the Windows 7 Professional or Ultimate editions, or Windows 8 Professional or Enterprise editions, you can open and edit the policies using the Local Group Policy Editor. To open the Local Group Policy Editor:

1. Press the Windows key, and then the letter R.
2. In the window that pops up, type "gpedit.msc." This opens the Local Group Policy Editor.

The group policies system is configured to apply policies either to a user or to a computer. After opening the Local Group Policy editor, you will see two policy sections, Computer Configuration and User Configuration. Computer configuration policies are applied to the targeted computer, and user configuration policies are applied to a specific user or group. In the Computer Configuration section, there are three major subsections:

Microsoft Local Group Policy Editor

- Software Settings
- Windows Settings
- Administrative Templates

In the User Configuration section, there are the same three subsections.

Administrative templates are extensions to the Windows policies. They add functionality to the policies for non-Windows applications like Chrome or Firefox. The administrative templates for Internet Explorer are included by default and are located under the computer or the user configurations. In the Administrative Templates option, go to Windows Components, then to the Internet Explorer option. To add administrative templates to the Local Group Policy Editor, download the appropriate files.

For Chrome:

1. Go to https://support.google.com/chrome/a/answer/187202?hl=en. Look for the link for the zip file for the Chrome templates.
2. Download them and unzip the files.
3. In the Policy Editor, right-click on Administrative Templates under Computer configuration or User configuration.

4. Choose Add/Remove Templates from the list and browse to the location where you saved the downloaded files. Browse to the windows/adm/en-us directory and choose the chrome.adm file.

5. After you return to the Policy Editor, expand the administrative templates folder under Computer

Administrative Template Addition

configuration or User configuration and open the Classic Administrative Templates folder. Under that you will find a folder called Google and then Google Chrome.

There are no official administrative templates for Firefox.

To modify a setting:

1. Find the settings you want to change. You can either browse the tree structure for the settings you want to change, or you can search for them. To search, right-click on the Administrative Templates option under Computer or User settings and choose Filter options.

2. Check the box next to Enable Keyword Filters and type your search term in the field.

3. Click on OK at the bottom of the page. The window will now display only the settings that have your search term in them.

4. Once you locate the setting you want to change, double-click on it to open the Settings box.

Filtering Options

5. From here, you can choose to not configure a setting, enable the setting, or disable the setting.

Each of these options has different functions depending on the setting. Each setting has a description box that details what the setting is, and what the options will do after they are set. Once you set an option, it takes effect immediately and can be tested right away. If Internet Explorer or Chrome is open at the time the setting is set, you may have to close and reopen the browser. Some settings, like the homepage setting, have boxes that allow you to specify the setting. The homepage setting allows you to force a default homepage for the browser that the user cannot change.

There are many options available for Internet Explorer and Chrome for both computer and user settings. For public computers in a library, there are some settings that would be useful to protect users' privacy. Each setting will be listed by name. To locate them, use the search feature. Depending on the version of the browser installed, not all settings may be available.

Internet Explorer Options

- **Do not allow users to enable or disable add-ons**—Enabling this option will prevent users from managing the add-ons.
- **Disable autocomplete**—This turns off Internet Explorer's ability to save data entered into forms and the location bar.
- **Turn off reopen last browsing session**—This will keep Internet Explorer from remembering the last browsing session.
- **Turn off browser geolocation**—With this enabled, the browser will not tell Internet servers where it is physically located.
- **Disable changing homepage settings**—With this enabled, you can set a homepage for the browser, and the user will be unable to change it.
- **Hide Favorites menu**—This turns off the Favorites menu. If a user saves a favorite, this will prevent it from being shown to other users.
- **Disable pages**—There are several options to prevent users from getting into the settings pages, including the advanced settings and the connections, general, programs, privacy, and security pages.
- **Always send Do Not Track header**—This forces Internet Explorer to request that sites do not track the user.
- **Empty temporary Internet files when browser is closed**—This does exactly as it states: when it is enabled, the browser clears its temporary files as soon as the browser is closed.

Chrome Options

- **Disable autofill**—Turning this off prevents users from being able to save data on the browser for automatically filling in forms.
- **Block third-party cookies**—Enabling this feature keeps the browser from accepting cookies from third-party servers.

- **Enable or disable bookmark editing**—This prevents users from being able to add or delete bookmarks.

- **Incognito mode availability**—Enabling this setting allows you to turn off or force Incognito mode.

- **Disable saving browser history**—Enabling this keeps the browser from saving the browsing history.

- **Configure home page**—With this, you can set the default homepage and prevent the user from changing it.

- **Enable the password manager**—Disabling this prevents the users from saving passwords for sites.

There are many more options and settings that can be set. It is a good idea to go through every setting and see what is available. Since the settings take effect immediately, it is easy to change a setting, then test it. If it does not work the way you wanted, then turn it off.

If you set policies for Internet Explorer or Chrome using the Local Group Policy Editor, then the settings you change will take effect for all users on the computer.

If you disable getting into the Internet Explorer settings, you as well as the user will then be unable to get into the settings. So, if you need to make changes to the settings, you will have to load the Local Group Policy Editor again and change that setting. If you are using the group policy editor in an Active Domain, then it is possible to set policies for users or groups.

Windows Applications

There are many applications available that can help libraries to secure public computers and to prevent personal or private information from being stored on the computers.

Deep Freeze

Deep Freeze is an application produced by a company called Faronics. When installed on a computer, Deep Freeze creates an image of the state of the software on the computer at the time it is turned on. As an individual uses the computer, any changes they make to the computer are treated as normal changes; but with Deep Freeze enabled, when the computer is rebooted, it reverts back to its previous state. This type of protection is fantastic in a public computer setting as it allows patrons to use the computer in a normal method. They are free to browse the Internet, save passwords, create bookmarks, log into personal sites, download files, and do almost anything else that people use computers for. When the patron is finished with the computer, it can be rebooted, and everything that the last patron did on the computer is gone.

The downside to Deep Freeze is that it is difficult to manage software on the computer since any changes that are made to it are temporary and will disappear when it is rebooted. System administrators who wish to update the browser software or perform Windows updates on the computer must first thaw the computer, or disable Deep Freeze and reboot the computer. After rebooting, the changes can be made to the computer; then it must be frozen or enabled again and rebooted. This process can be simplified using the enterprise version of the software, which allows the administrator to thaw and update a group of computers at one time.

Using the standard version of Deep Freeze is pretty straightforward. After purchasing the software, boot up the computer you want to install it on. It is important that all the settings you want to have set on the computer are set before you install the software. This includes any browser settings, security settings, policies, and application settings you want the computer to have for each new user. This is a great chance to run the Windows Update to make sure the computer is up-to-date on all the security updates. Also make sure that the antivirus application has the most recent definition files. Once the computer settings are set the way you want them to be, go ahead and install Deep Freeze by running through the Deep Freeze installation wizard.

1. On the installer page, click on Next, then accept the license terms.
2. On the next page, you will need to put in your license key that you received from Faronics.
3. The next page asks what drive on the computer you want to freeze. The box next to the C drive should be checked.
4. Click on Next to continue. The last page summarizes the installation process.
5. Click on the Install button to install the application.
6. After the installation ends, the computer will restart and it will be "frozen." The only visible indication that the computer is frozen is the Deep Freeze icon in the task bar. The icon looks like the face of a polar bear.

You can open the Deep Freeze administration console by holding down the Ctrl key, the Alt key, the Shift key, then tapping the F6 key. This will prompt you for the Deep Freeze console password. There is no password initially. From the console, you can choose to thaw the computer on the next restart and then freeze it again after the

Deep Freeze Console

next reboot, or thaw the computer and keep it thawed until you freeze it again. To thaw the computer, select the box next to Boot Thawed. When you click on OK, the program will prompt you to reboot. From that point on, the computer will be thawed and any changes will be kept. To freeze it again, open the console and choose Boot Frozen. Again, the program will prompt you to reboot, and now it will be frozen again. You can choose to boot the computer thawed for only a few restarts by choosing the Boot Thawed on Next option and picking how many restarts you want to have thawed.

It is good practice to thaw Deep Freeze computers every week or two to run Windows updates and to update definition files on the antivirus application. Many applications, such as Firefox, Chrome, Java, Flash, and Acrobat, will also need updates. If you have a network, it is useful to thaw a computer, run the updates from a network drive, and then freeze the computer again. If you don't have a network, you can copy the update files to a USB drive or burn them to a CD to take around to the individual computers.

Disk Cleanup

Using Windows creates junk files all over the computer. As mentioned before, using Internet browsers creates temporary files, but installing applications also creates temporary files, as does running applications. These files are stored in various locations on the computer, and not all of them are easy to find and clean. The Windows registry is a dynamic place where entries are created, modified, and deleted frequently. As these changes are made to the registry, sometimes they are not deleted, or they are incorrectly changed. This happens when the application that made the registry changes was unable to remove them or just did not try to delete them. As Windows is running, it must keep the registry loaded in memory, and the more complex the registry becomes, the slower Windows becomes, and the more users will experience issues with it loading incorrect entries.

Fortunately, Microsoft provides a way to clean the temporary files from the computer. You can access the Disk Cleanup wizard for the drive from the Properties window.

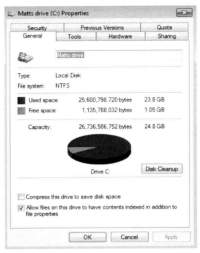

Disk Options Window

1. Open Windows Explorer and right-click on the drive you want to clean up.

2. On the first tab, General, there is a summary of the drive including its name, size, how much of the drive is being used, some options for compressing unused files, and an option for indexing files on the drive.

3. You will also see a button called Disk Cleanup. Clicking on this button opens a small window that runs for a few minutes and calculates the amount of space that will be restored by running the cleanup activity. At this time, the application is not deleting any files, but simply gathering a report of what files it can delete.

4. The next window that opens shows the list of categories of files that can be deleted and how much space will be restored. There are several categories including downloaded program files, temporary Internet files, offline webpages, error reporting files, the recycle bin, temporary files, and image thumbnails. You can check or uncheck each category as desired.

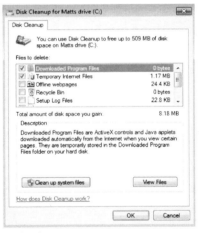

Disk Cleanup

5. Once you click OK, the system will actually delete the files.

This is a useful tool to run before you freeze a computer with Deep Freeze. This cleans up the computer and does not leave behind any personal or private information in the temporary files or temporary Internet files.

The problem with the Microsoft Disk Cleanup utility is that it is only aware of the Microsoft applications installed on the computer. This means that any programs that are not from Microsoft, such as Chrome, Firefox, or Java, may still store private information and will not have their temporary files cleared when this utility is run. For this reason, it is recommended you clear those applications' caches directly through the application or run a utility that clears them all at once. (Clearing the temporary caches for Chrome and Firefox is covered in chapter 3.) Other applications like Acrobat, Java, and many others store their own temporary files in separate locations, some of which may include personal or private information. Each program has its own unique way to clear caches.

CCleaner

The fastest and easiest way to clear the temporary files for all the applications at once is to use a separate utility like CCleaner. CCleaner is an application from the company Piriform and can be found at www.piri form.com. The application is available in a free version and a paid version. The difference between the two versions is that the free version does not include automatic updating, file recovery, real-time monitoring, and some other features.

After downloading the CCleaner application, double-click on it to install it.

1. Choose your language and click Next.

2. The program comes with several options for installation. You can choose the default, which is to

CCleaner Install Wizard

put an icon on the desktop and the Start menu, add the option to run CCleaner to the Right-click menu for the recycle bin, automatically check to see if there are any updates for CCleaner when you start the application, and if you want to enable the intelligent cookie scan. The intelligent cookie scan is a system that is aware of cookies from certain sites and can keep those cookies. This is useful if you are using a personal computer and want to maintain the site preferences and login information for sites you use often. This is not a useful feature for a public computer, since it may keep logins for private websites. This allows a user to see the personal information of previous users on the computer.

3. After picking your options, click Install to continue. When installation is done, leave the option to run CCleaner checked and uncheck the View Release Notes option.

The main CCleaner interface opens. From this screen, you can access the main features of the application. CCleaner has three main activities:

- Cleaner
- Registry
- Tools

The Cleaner option scans the computer for files that can be deleted off the computer. It is possible to clean the temporary files, cookies, history, recently typed-in sites, and download history for Internet Explorer, Firefox, and Chrome. It can also clear recent documents, empty the recycle bin, clear system temporary files, delete old error reporting files, clear old log files, and perform many more cleaning activities from the Windows operating system. Under the Applications tab at the top, it can also clear temporary files from a variety of applications including PDF applications like Acrobat, antivirus applications, Microsoft Office, Adobe Flash Player, and many more depending on what applications are installed on the computer.

CCleaner Interface

NOTE: Before running the cleaner, make sure you review the list of all the cleaning that the program will do. If there is an application or an option that you do not want to have cleared, uncheck that option.

CCleaner Clean Analysis

There are two ways to run the cleaner. You can either *analyze* the computer or *run* the cleaner. Analyze goes through the system, gathering the list of the files that can be cleaned. It then presents a list of all the cleaning activities it can make. It shows what the application is, how much space it will free up, and how many files will be removed. The other way that the cleaner can run is to simply run the cleaner. This does not show a list of the changes that will be made; it just deletes the files and shows a report of the changes it made after the fact.

To run the Analyze function:

1. Click on the Analyze button at the bottom left of the application screen. The system will run from a few seconds up to a few minutes. When it is done, it presents a list of the changes it will make.
2. If you are happy with the changes, click on the Run Cleaner button.
3. If you want to make changes to the applications or files it is cleaning, you can uncheck or check the options in the menu at the left, and then click the Analyze button again. This causes it to run through the system again and present a revised list of changes.
4. After you click on the Run Cleaner option, it will remove those files from the system and show a summary of the changes it made to the system.

NOTE: Before clicking the Run Cleaner option, make sure that the changes you want to make on the computer are changes you really want to make. Once the cleaner runs and deletes files, there is no undo. The files are not moved into the recycle bin and cannot be restored.

The Registry option scans through the Windows registry, looks for problems or errors in the registry, and presents a list of changes. The types of errors CCleaner can detect and fix include issues with application paths, abandoned file extensions, and unused entries. Unused entries are leftover settings from programs that are no longer installed or settings that are left behind after applications are uninstalled.

To run a registry scan:

1. Click on the Scan for Issues button at the bottom left. The program will scan and return a list of suggested changes.

CC Registry Cleaner

2. Review the changes CCleaner suggests by scrolling up and down the lists. By default the program will delete all the identified problems, but you can choose to not delete an identified problem by unchecking the box next to that line.
3. Once you have reviewed all the problems, click on the Fix Selected Issues button on the bottom right. The system will ask if you want

to make a backup of the changes it is going to make before it makes them. This is a safety feature to protect your computer from inadvertently making changes that adversely affect the way your computer operates. Since the registry is one of the most important pieces of the Windows operating system, and any changes to the registry can cause major issues, it is strongly recommended that you back up the registry before the changes are made.

4. Choosing "yes" allows you to save the file to a location on the computer. The file should have a .reg extension. To make it easier to restore the file to a public computer should it be needed, the file should be given a file name that makes sense and is easily identifiable, such as public1-Jan012014.reg. If a problem is identified that requires you to restore the registry files from CCleaner, simply double-click on the .reg file you wish to restore and answer yes to the prompt that asks if you want to merge the changes into the registry.

5. After saving the backup, CCleaner will show you each of the identified problems and ask you what you want to do with each one. The prompt shows the problem, a suggested solution, and a couple of options for fixing it.

6. Clicking on the Fix Issue button performs the suggested solution for that problem. Clicking on the Fix All Selected Issues button performs the suggested solution for every checked problem.

CCleaner Registry Fix Options

7. After running the registry scan the first time, run the scan again a second or even a third time until CCleaner shows there are no identified problems.

The Tools option has several features for simply configuring Windows applications on the computer. The first option is Uninstall. This is the same as the Windows system uninstall process located in the Control Panel, but it offers a few extra features including the ability to delete a program from the uninstall list, but leave it on the computer. The Startup option shows a list of all the programs that start up on the computer when it is booted. It is not always apparent what programs are launched when the computer starts, since many of them are running in the background of the computer without your knowledge. This feature is useful for

CCleaner Uninstall Options

identifying possible spyware applications that may be installed on the computer. The list of applications shows if they are enabled or not. If they are enabled, they will run; if you disable one, it will remain in the list, but it will not be started when the computer starts.

The Startup option also shows the key of where the program is being started from. Programs can be started from several locations on the computer including the registry and the startup folder. The Program column shows the name of the program and the publisher, which is the company that makes that program. The last column shows the location and name of the program that will be run. This list is usually full of different programs that need to be run when the computer starts, includ-

CCleaner Startup Options

ing drivers for the network card or other computer hardware; update programs for Java, Acrobat, or other programs; and programs that put access to a program in the taskbar next to the clock. If there are any entries you are not sure of in the list, you can disable them by clicking on the item in the list, and then clicking on the Disable button on the right. After you disable an item, restart the computer and make sure everything is running properly. If you need to reenable the item, click on it again and click on the Enable button. If you are sure you want to remove a program from the list and prevent it from running when the computer starts, click on it, then click on the Delete button. This will remove it from the list.

Keep in mind that if you reinstall or update an application that has entries in the startup list, it will most likely restore those entries as well. For example, the Java application has an update application that is installed to run at startup. If you disable or delete the Java updater and then later install a newer version, the installer will restore or reenable the update application. If there are entries in the startup that you do not recognize or that you suspect may be unwanted applications, look for the corresponding entry in the Uninstall feature, or search for the executable file on the Internet. Most spyware applications that run on the computer by placing entries in the startup list are known, and by searching for them on the Internet you can confirm that it is safe to remove them from the list.

The File Finder feature allows you to search the computer for duplicate files. You can specify what directories or drives to search, exclude files based on size, and ignore system or hidden files. When you click on the Search button, the system returns a list of all the files it has identified that have identical copies. Check the box next to the files you want to delete and click on the Delete Selected button.

> **NOTE:** Do not remove any files from the computer unless you are sure that the duplicates are not needed. If you are unsure, search the Internet for that application or file.

The System Restore option shows you the list of the system restore points that were created on the computer. Whenever a major change is made to the computer, it creates a system restore point. These system restore points are useful in case you make a change to the computer or install an application that misbehaves and causes problems. To restore the computer to a working state, try reverting it to a previous restore point. Keep in mind that restore files take up space and can be deleted. The System Restore option in CCleaner shows all the system restore points that exist on your computer, which can be removed by clicking on one and clicking the Remove button.

The last option on the Tools menu is the Drive Wiper. The idea behind the drive wiper is to clean the free space on the computer, or to completely wipe an existing drive. When files are deleted from the hard drive on the computer, they are not really removed, they are simply marked as being deleted. When the system needs more disk space to write files, it can use space that has been marked as deleted by files that are no longer needed. This means that it is possible for a program to view files that are on the computer that have been marked as deleted, but are still on the computer. With the right program, the files can be undeleted and viewed. This could be used to view personal or private information about previous users on the computer. Using CCleaner, you can wipe the free space on the computer, making it harder or impossible to restore and view deleted files.

CCleaner Drive Wiper

CCleaner does this by writing useless data to the areas of the disk that are marked as being free. Every time the free space is written over, it becomes harder to restore the information that was there previously. In other words, the more times the data is overwritten, the more difficult it is to see the original information.

To wipe the free space:

1. Make sure that Free Space Only is in the Wipe field and choose the level of security you want to wipe. Simple Overwrite will write to the free space once, and Very Complex Overwrite will write to the free space 35 times. Keep in mind that the speed of the wipe depends on the size of the hard drive, the amount of free space, and the number of writes. The bigger the drive, the more free space, and more writes will take longer.

2. Choose the drive you wish to wipe and click on the Wipe button. The program will show an update bar as it is wiping the drive; and when it is complete, it will show a confirmation that it has finished.

For public computers, CCleaner can be automated to run at specified times. This can be done in several ways. Using the Windows Task Scheduler is an efficient and easy way to schedule CCleaner to run at specified times.

Windows Task Scheduler

To access the Task Scheduler:

1. Open the control panel, then open the Administrative Tools option.

2. Next, open the Task Scheduler. From the Task Scheduler window, click on the Task Scheduler Library on the left side, and then click on Create Basic Task on the right side of the window.

3. The program will open a task wizard.

4. On the first page, give the task a name like "CCleaner daily" and a description like "Run CCleaner daily at 2 pm."

5. Click Next. On the next page, you can choose when you want the task to run. You can choose daily, weekly, monthly, one time, when the computer starts, when the user logs in, or when a specified event is logged. For a CCleaner task you could have it run once a day during the time the library is open. You could also have it run every day when the user logs in.

6. For this example, choose Daily and then Next.

7. On the next page, specify what day and time you want the task to run, then choose the recurrence. The default is every 1 day.

8. Click Next. On the next page, choose what action you want the task to perform.

9. Choose Start a Program and click Next.

10. Click on the Browse button and find the executable file for CCleaner. On most computers it will be located at C:\program files \ccleaner\ccleaner.exe. To make CCleaner run in the background without user interference, type /AUTO in the Add Arguments box.

11. Click Next.

12. The program will display a summary of the task.

13. If you are satisfied with the options, click Finish.

If the user that is regularly logged into the computer does not have administrative rights to the system, you will need to change what users run the CCleaner task from the General tab for the task.

New Task Summary

1. Double-click on the task to open it.

2. Change the User Account option on the General tab to "Run with the Highest Privileges." This gives the CCleaner application the directive to run and clean files even though the user does not have the rights to do it.

3. Now, every day at 2 pm, the system will run the CCleaner executable file in the background, perform the basic cleaning activities, and close without user intervention.

Some computer reservation programs used by libraries have the ability to run applications when a user starts a session or when a session ends. For PC Reservation:

1. Open the options from the menu, then click on the Programs tab.

2. On "Run These Applications at Session End," type in the command to run CCleaner automatically: C:\program files\ccleaner\ccleaner .exe /AUTO.

3. Now, when the user's session ends, the computer will run the CCleaner application, remove all the temporary Internet files, and clear the recycle bin and the system temp files.

There are a variety of other ways that CCleaner can be run automatically using more advanced applications. For example, it is possible to have a scripting application run when the browser is closed to clean the temporary files, history, and downloads just for that browser.

Proxies and The Onion Router (Tor)

When communicating on the Internet, one of the safest ways to transmit information is to use a proxy server. A proxy server is a type of online server that gathers requests for a client and makes the requests to the server for the client. After receiving the information from the server, the proxy then sends the data to the client. This way, the client and the server are separated from each other since the proxy sits between them. While communicating this way, the server "believes" the client is the proxy server, not the actual client. This protects the client from the server and from any kind of tracking it may do based on the IP address of the client or fingerprinting. The proxy server can be configured to strip out identifiable information from the client's requests and block potentially dangerous cookies and beacons from the server's communication. The best type of proxy to use for browsing the Internet is a web proxy. A web proxy is a webpage a user visits, typing in the name of the website they want to view. The web proxy will request the page for the user and return the page to the user.

There are many web proxies on the Internet that can be used to make a user's Internet traffic anonymous. Some have subscription costs, but there are some free services as well. Anonymouse.org is one site that offers a free web proxy. From the www.anonymouse.org site, type in the webpage you want to see and click on Surf Anonymously. The proxy will grab the website and return it in the same way as if you had requested it normally. If you

Anonymouse.org Example

look at the location bar, you will notice that the URL shows it is being requested and returned through the anonymouse.org site.

Another site that offers free web proxy services is www.ninjaproxy. com. This site allows the user to block cookies and remove scripts from requested sites. It operates the same way: Type in the webpage you want to see, choose if you want to block cookies or scripts, then click on Go. The proxy will retrieve the site and return it to you. Ninja Proxy also allows you to choose to force a secure connection.

Ninja Proxy

Web proxies do have weaknesses. Users at public computers could use web proxies to protect their surfing habits online, but the local computer would still have caches of sites that were visited, and these sites could be viewed by other users.

Using a web proxy slows down communication, since there is additional time spent having another server make the requests for the client. Proxies are also not the most reliable form of communication. Since there is only one server, the web proxy can become busy or too overloaded to respond in a timely manner, or it can even fail. Web proxies come and go, so their availability is not always dependable. Public computers could be configured to connect to a web proxy when they are opened, or a list of web proxies could be provided to patrons when they log into the computer or when they open a webpage.

The Onion Router, or Tor, is a specialized network of connected servers on the Internet called "relays." Each relay is connected to other relays using an encrypted connection. Relays are located in every corner of the world, so any communication passing between them is routed all over. A user who is connected to the Tor network has a high level of protection since that communication is passed between relays hundreds of times. Every time a relay passes the communication, it is encrypted and passed to another encrypted relay. Eventually, the communication leaves the Tor network at an exit node and the destination server is contacted. The response back from the server is then routed back through the Tor network, using another random path back to the original user. It is practically impossible for the destination server to know who made the original request or where that request is going. It is also extremely difficult for another user on the Internet to see where the traffic of a particular user is coming from or where it is going due to the dynamic and encrypted nature of the Tor network.

The name for The Onion Router comes from the many layers of encryption that are added to any communication that travels through it. It is similar to the layers of an onion.

Tor is used by anyone who wants to have their communication on the Internet be as private as possible. Journalists traveling in hostile countries or who do not want their communication eavesdropped on use the Tor network for communication back to the United States. It is also used by political activists or by ordinary citizens in countries that censor the Internet. It is a known tool used by former NSA contractor Edward Snowden to communicate with news outlets.

Tor is available as a specialized version of the Firefox browser. The Firefox browser is preconfigured to connect to the Tor network, and it is configured in such a way as to maximize the privacy features of the Firefox browser and to protect the user's online anonymity. The Tor browser can be downloaded from the Tor website: www.torproject.org. To install it, simply run the downloaded installation file. The only option you have during install is to choose an install location. Once it is installed, you can move the directory that Tor was installed into anywhere. It can be placed on a USB drive to be used anywhere, including on public computers.

Using Tor

Once Tor is downloaded and installed, run the executable file called Start Tor Browser.exe. The first time you run it, Tor will ask you how you want to connect. The most common way is to connect using the normal connection option. The second option is for advanced connection options for special situations. For instance, if your network required a special configuration to route traffic to the Internet like an internal proxy server, then you would need to use the second option and specify the proxy information. In most cases, this is not required, and the normal connection options can be used.

Tor Network Settings

Once the program has started, it displays a connection page, showing that it is connected to the Tor network and it is ready to go.

To check whether the Tor browser is using the Tor network and to show that the network is properly masking your IP address, go to the website www.whatismyipaddress.com. This site shows you the IP address that you are currently appearing as on the Internet and where that IP address is located.

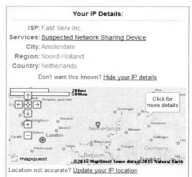

WhatIsMyIpAddress.com Example

Google Nederland. Google and the Google logo are registered trademarks of Google Inc., used with permission.

As you browse the Internet using the Tor browser, your IP address changes. So, if you visit the www.whatismyipaddress.com site again, it will show a different IP address. Another way to see that the Tor browser is working is to view a website that changes its features or its interface based on the IP address. Google displays in different ways, including in a different language, based on the IP address.

While you are browsing the Web using the Tor browser, it is not keeping a history of sites that you visit, nor is it keeping a cache of downloaded Internet files. When you close the Tor browser, there are no traces left of where your browser went.

The biggest weakness of the Tor network is the unencrypted connections exiting the Tor network. All the communication inside the network is encrypted, but it is not encrypted at the point where it exits the network. So, it is possible for the remote site traffic to be monitored and logged.

Also, anyone can operate a relay on the network. If any one relay on the network were attempting to monitor or log users passing through it, it is possible they would be able to see a certain IP address using the network. Since the traffic is encrypted, they would not be able to see what sites were being accessed.

Even though the Tor network seems to operate in an illegal way, it is perfectly legal to operate and use the Tor network. Using the Tor network or providing the Tor browser to patrons is perfectly legal.

Antivirus and Spyware Applications

Running an up-to-date, current antivirus application is vital to the operation of any computer. Antivirus applications protect the computer against viruses that can damage the software on the computer, cause havoc on a network, and potentially infect other computers; these applications also protect against spyware, which can potentially monitor and give away personal information like browsing behavior, not to mention other types of malicious software that can damage the computer or steal private information.

MICROSOFT SECURITY ESSENTIALS

There are several free antivirus applications that protect against viruses and spyware. Microsoft offers a free solution called Microsoft Security Essentials. Security Essentials works only on Windows 7 and Vista.

To download MS Security Essentials: Go to http://windows.microsoft .com/en-us/windows/security-essentials-download and click on the download link.

1. After downloading the installer, run it.
2. Click Next on the first screen and click "I accept" on the Licensing Terms page.
3. The next page asks if you want to join the customer experience improvement program. After choosing, click on Next to go to the Optimize screen. The customer improvement program is used by Microsoft to improve the Security Essentials program. It collects data about how you use the program and sends it to Microsoft. There is a link to the privacy statement on the screen so you can review it before opting in.
4. This page has two options, whether to turn on the Windows firewall, and whether you want to have files that are marked as viruses sent to Microsoft for more analysis.
5. The firewall should definitely be turned on, so check the Firewall option.
6. Then decide whether or not you want to turn on Sample Submission. If Security Essentials determines that an application may be potentially dangerous, it could send the information about that program to Microsoft. Microsoft will do some further investigation into the program and make a determination if it is dangerous or not. Any new information about programs submitted through the sample submission program are included in updates to the Security Essentials program. Participation in this program is voluntary. It is not necessary to use Sample Submissions, and I recommend that you turn it off.
7. Next, the installer warns you that having other antispyware programs on your computer may interfere with the operation of Microsoft Security Essentials. It is generally not a good idea to have more than one antivirus or antispyware application running on a computer at one time. They may see each other as potentially dangerous and interfere with operations.

8. Once the application is installed, run it to force it to update to the latest virus and spyware information and to run an initial scan of the computer.

The application will monitor files as they are written to the computer and when any files are read from the computer. If it sees anything that matches a pattern in its database, it will alert you.

Microsoft Security Essentials Initial Scan

Security Essentials Protected Screen

When you open the Security Essentials screen, it shows whether the application is up to date by displaying a green bar at the top. If the bar is red, it means that the application is out of date, or it has not run a scan in a long time.

You can force the application to run a scan by clicking on the Scan Now button, then choosing a quick, full, or custom scan. A quick scan scans only certain areas of the computer where viruses and spyware typically are installed. A full scan takes longer to perform, but it scans the entire computer. The custom scan gives you the option to specify what drives and directories you want to scan. This is useful if you want to scan only an external drive, or only one directory on the computer. At the top of the window, you'll see several tabs. The second tab is the Update tab. On this tab you can see when the latest database updates for viruses and spyware were downloaded. You can also force the application to update to the newest versions right now by clicking on the Update button.

The History tab shows a list of all the items the program has identified as being quarantined, allowed, and detected. Quarantined items are known viruses and spyware files that the application identified and stored in a temporary location on the computer. Allowed items are all the files that the application allowed to run; and detected items are all the items the system detected, including quarantined items and deleted items.

The Settings tab offers options to schedule when the application will perform scans, settings for turning off protection, and different ways to exclude the scanner. The first option sets the schedule for the scan. By default the system performs a weekly quick scan of the computer on Sundays. You can change to a different schedule by changing the options. The next option is the default actions for when the application detects a threat. You can set a different action for each threat level, severe, high,

Security Essentials Settings

medium, and low. You can have the system remove or delete the file, or quarantine it. The medium and low levels also have the option to allow the file or process to continue. In the excluded files, locations, and types, you can specify what areas of the computer you do not want to scan. The last option, called MAPS, is a service that the app offers to automatically send information to Microsoft about potentially harmful software on your computer. By default, the app is configured to send some information to Microsoft.

Windows Defender

If you are running Windows 8, you cannot run Security Essentials. Instead, Microsoft has another free application called Windows Defender. Defender is basically the same application as Security Essentials and has the same interface. To locate it in Windows 8, open the Start screen, click on the Search option, and type in Defender. From the result list, choose Windows Defender. The operation and configuration of Windows Defender is the same as previously described for Security Essentials.

Windows 8 Search Screen

AVG

Another free antivirus and antispyware application is AVG. It is available at http://free.avg.com. It is available in a pay version as well that adds more services like download protection, encryption, antispam for email, and a firewall.

To install AVG:

1. Download the installer and launch it.

2. After preparing itself for a minute, the installer will ask you what language you want to use.

3. Choose your language and click Next.

4. The next page is the end user license agreement. After reviewing it, click on the Accept button.

5. The next screen shows you the additional features you will gain if you purchase the paid version. Choose the basic edition and click on Next.

6. Even though you are using the free version, you still need a license number. The installer will automatically create a license key for you if you chose the free edition.

7. Click Next.

8. Next, the installer will ask you if you want to use the express or custom install. Leave the option for the express install and click on Next.

9. The installer then downloads the files needed for installation and installs them, so it may take a few minutes for it to complete.

10. When it is done, it will ask you to reboot your computer. After rebooting, you can open the interface by double-clicking on the AVG icon.

AVG Main Screen

AVG Scheduled Scan Settings

From the main interface, you can run a full scan of the computer by clicking on the Scan Now button. The system will scan the computer and return with a report showing any detected problems. You can customize the settings for the scan including a schedule by clicking on the gear next to the Scan Now button. From here, you can click on Manage Scheduled Scans to view the current schedules and edit them. By default, AVG includes a scheduled scan that is disabled. To enable it, click on the scheduled scan, then on the Edit Schedule button.

To enable the scan, click on the red Disabled icon. It should turn green and say Enabled. Now you can change the settings. You can choose when the scan runs, either hourly, daily at a specified time, or on computer startup.

The Settings option on the left allows you to set more specific settings for the scan.

- **Heal/Remove Virus Infections without Asking Me**—This option automatically cleans or fixes infections without asking for permission.

- **Report Potentially Unwanted Programs and Spyware Threats**—Enabling this option turns on the antispyware features of AVG. It scans the computer for spyware applications that may be dangerous and reports them.

- **Report Enhanced Set of Potentially Unwanted Programs**—With this option enabled, the AVG scanner scans for more spyware applications and reports them. Using this option could potentially cause AVG to report applications you want on the computer as potentially dangerous. Some free applications like games or utilities include features that make them appear to be spyware. AVG could report them as dangerous.

- **Scan for Tracking Cookies**—This option searches the computer for cookies that are tracking the user and removes them. This is a great option for public computers.

- **Scan Inside Archives**—If there are any files on the computer that are inside compressed archives, they are not scanned by default, but with this option checked, they will be scanned.

- **Use Heuristics**—As AVG scans the computer, it compares files against a list of known threats. With heuristics turned on, the program will attempt to identify unknown threats by looking at the files on the computer. If a file appears to be a threat, it will be identified.

- **Scan System Environment**—This forces AVG to scan all the currently running programs, any applications forced to run automatically, and any drivers running. Since many spyware applications run in memory or are run at startup, this option increases the likelihood that they will be identified.

- **Enable Thorough Scanning**—Enabling this option forces AVG to scan every part of the computer, including areas of the computer that are rarely infected in any way. This option slows down the scanning process, but it ensures that there are no infections anywhere on the computer.

- **Scan for Rootkits**—A rootkit is a malicious type of spyware that is installed on the computer in a way that causes it to run before Windows loads. Since the rootkit is running before Windows loads, it is difficult for the operating system to be aware of it. Rootkits are used for a variety of reasons by hackers. They can be used to steal private information about the user or use the computer to send out viruses or spam. Enabling this option will force the scanner to look for rootkits on the computer. *This option should always be checked.*

The last option on the left side, Location, allows you to specify where on the computer to scan. You can specify what drives to scan by default or what drives or directories to not scan.

After you have configured the scan settings the way you want, click on the Save button to return to the Scheduled Scans screen.

AVG will attempt to update the virus and spyware definition files automatically. If for some reason they are out of date, the program will report that the system is not protected. To force the program to update to the most recent version of the program and the antivirus and antispyware definition files, click on the Update Now button.

There are many ways to configure public computers to provide more security and protection for library users. Many of them also increase the privacy of the users on the computers. Start simply and safely by adding antivirus and antispam applications to the computers. Not only do they provide simple privacy features, but these applications also increase the security of the computers and add to the overall safety of the library network. Every computer on a network must have an antivirus and anti-spam application on it. Once these are installed and working well, create a plan to keep them up-to-date and ensure that they are getting updates frequently, at least once a week. Then start adding more security for your users by offering secure and private browsing with the addition of the Tor browser, or provide links to web proxies. Create a schedule or an automatic way to clean the computers regularly to keep personal and private information off them and to keep them running efficiently. If additional privacy is needed or you have a large number of public computers to manage, look into the possibility of adding computer policies.

Bibliography

AVG. "AVG Antivirus Free FAQ." Accessed December 20, 2014, http://support.avg .com/support_Free?retURL=support_win

Digital Trends. "A Beginner's Guide to Tor: How to Navigate through the Underground Internet." Last modified August 15, 2014, http://www.digitaltrends.com/com puting/a-beginners-guide-to-tor-how-to-navigate-through-the-underground -internet/

Faronics. "Deep Freeze Manual." Accessed December 20, 2014, http://www.faronics .com/assets/DFS_Manual.pdf

How-To-Geek. "How to Browse Anonymously with TOR." Last modified May 15, 2012, http://www.howtogeek.com/114004/how-to-browse-anonymously-with-tor/

How-To-Geek. "How to Use CCleaner Like a Pro." Accessed December 2014, http:// www.howtogeek.com/113382/how-to-use-ccleaner-like-a-pro-9-tips-tricks/

Microsoft. "Group Policy for Beginners." Last modified April 27, 2011, http://technet .microsoft.com/en-us/library/hh147307%28v=ws.10%29.aspx

Microsoft. "Rootkits." Accessed December 20, 2014, http://www.microsoft.com/secu rity/portal/mmpc/threat/rootkits.aspx

Piriform. "Using CCleaner." Accessed December 20, 2014, https://www.piriform.com /docs/ccleaner/using-ccleaner

Webopedia. "Rootkit." Accessed December 20, 2014, http://www.webopedia.com /TERM/R/rootkit.html

CHAPTER 6

Browser Settings and Plug-Ins

Browser Settings

The most commonly used browsers are Microsoft's Internet Explorer, Mozilla Firefox, and Google Chrome. Each of these browsers has strengths and weaknesses. Internet Explorer is preinstalled with most copies of Windows, and it is fairly easy to use. It also has a history of not being the fastest browser, and until most recently, it wasn't the easiest to add features to. Firefox has become very popular in recent years, mainly since it is quite fast and easy to extend. There are thousands of extensions and add-ons available for Firefox that add features and functionality to it. Definitely one of the biggest strengths of Firefox is the community that develops additional software for it. Firefox has been losing ground recently to Google Chrome. Chrome is very lightweight in that it is very small and fast to install. It is very quick when browsing the Internet. One of the biggest complaints about Chrome is its strong tie-in with Google and its products. Chrome, when it is logged into a Google account, keeps track of everything and allows users to keep their favorites and open webpages saved and have access to them from other computers. This feature is fantastic for personal use, but it is not desirable in a public computer situation since it exposes one user's personal information to other users.

There are ways to control the way that the browsers operate on public computers. It is possible to control the features of the browsers in order to prevent them from keeping users' personal information or from sending out identifiable information. All three browsers also offer the ability to extend their abilities and features to provide more functionality. For public computers, it is possible to install plug-ins on browsers that add the ability to browse more privately or to remove personally identifying information.

Privacy Mode

All three of the major Internet browsers offer a privacy mode. This is a special type of mode that attempts to protect the user's privacy by not storing browsing data like cookies and temporary files. When the user closes the privacy mode, the system clears all the cookies and temporary files that were used during that session. The browser does not keep a history of sites visited.

Internet Explorer InPrivate Mode

Internet Explorer version 11 offers InPrivate mode. This mode does not keep any history or temporary files. Since some extensions and plug-ins can store personal information and may store temporary files or put cookies on the computer, the InPrivate mode disables all extensions by default. If there are any other browser add-ons like toolbars, they are also disabled.

Internet Explorer InPrivate Mode

While you are in the InPrivate mode, the browser shows the words "InPrivate" next to the location bar. To exit InPrivate mode, simply close all InPrivate windows.

On public computers it is possible to launch Internet Explorer in InPrivate mode every time the computer is started up. The simplest way to do this is to create an icon on the desktop for the user that launches into InPrivate mode. To create an icon that does this:

1. Start by finding the Internet Explorer icon on the start menu.
2. Right-click on it and choose Send to—Desktop (create shortcut). This puts an Internet Explorer icon on the desktop.
3. If you are using Windows 8, find the Internet Explorer icon on the start screen, right-click on it, and choose Open location.
4. From the window that opens, right-click on the Internet Explorer icon and choose Send to—Desktop (create shortcut).
5. Find the icon on the desktop, right-click on it, and choose Properties.
6. On the Shortcut tab, locate the Target box. It should read something like: "C:\Program Files\Internet Explorer\iexplore.exe"
7. At the end of it, add "–private" to it so that it reads: "C:\Program Files\Internet Explorer\iexplore.exe" – private

8. On the General tab, change the title to something descriptive like Internet Explorer Private Mode. Once that icon has been launched, it always opens Internet Explorer in InPrivate mode.

Firefox Private Browsing

Firefox's private mode is called Private Browsing. Firefox's Private Browsing mode is the same as Internet Explorer's InPrivate mode. When it's operating, the computer does not store any history, cookies, or temporary files. To open Private Browsing mode, click on the Firefox menu and choose New Private Window. The window that opens shows that it is in Private Browsing mode by displaying a purple mask icon in the upper left side of the window. To exit Private Browsing mode, close all the Private Browsing windows and tabs.

Internet Explorer Icon Settings

Firefox Private Browsing Mode

To have Firefox automatically launch into Private Browsing mode:

1. Start by creating a new icon on the desktop. Find the Firefox icon on the Start menu, right-click on it, and choose Send to—Desktop (create shortcut).

2. If you are using Windows 8, find the Firefox icon on the Start menu, right-click on it, and choose Open File Location.

3. In the window that opens, find the Firefox program, right-click on it, and choose Send to—Desktop (create shortcut).

4. Go back to the desktop, find the newly created Firefox icon, and right-click on it. Choose Properties.

5. On the Shortcut tab, locate the Target box. It should read something like this: "C:\Program Files (x86)\Mozilla Firefox\firefox.exe"

6. To the end of this, add "–private" so that it looks like this: "C:\Program Files (x86)\Mozilla Firefox\firefox.exe" – private

7. On the General tab, change the name of the icon to something descriptive like Mozilla Firefox—Private mode.

Now when this icon is launched it will open Firefox in Private Browsing mode.

Firefox Privacy Settings

Firefox also allows you to set the browser to always operate in Private Browsing mode.

1. Open the Firefox settings by clicking on the Firefox menu, then open Options.

2. From the Options box, click on the Privacy tab at the top.

3. Drop down the menu next to "Firefox will" in the History section.

4. Choose the option to "Use custom settings for history."

5. Below this, several options will open. Check the box next to the first option—"Always use Private Browsing mode."

With this option checked, Firefox will always open and operate in Private Browsing mode.

Chrome Incognito Mode

Google Chrome offers a privacy mode called incognito mode. As with privacy settings on Internet Explorer and Firefox, when Chrome is in incognito mode, it will not remember any browsing history, keep any temporary files, or accept any cookies. It will also disable any extensions that are installed in Chrome. It does this since some extensions gather private information and record browsing history. If you want to enable an extension to run in incognito mode:

1. Click on the Chrome menu button, then on Settings. Chrome will open a new tab with the settings.

2. On the left side, click on Extensions to display a list of the installed extensions.

3. Find the extension you want to enable in incognito mode and check the box next to it that says "Allow in incognito."

Chrome Extensions

4. Any currently open incognito windows will have to be closed and opened again to enable that extension.

Chrome displays a small icon of a man wearing a hat in the upper left corner of the application to show that the browser is in incognito mode. To exit incognito mode, close all the open incognito tabs and windows.

You can also create an icon that launches into incognito mode:

Chrome Incognito Mode. Google and the Google logo are registered trademarks of Google Inc., used with permission.

1. Click on the Start menu, find the Chrome icon, right-click on it, and choose Send to—Desktop (create shortcut).

2. If you are using Windows 8, locate the Chrome icon on the Start screen, right-click on it, and choose Open File Location.

3. In the window that opens, right-click on the Chrome icon and choose Send to—Desktop (create shortcut).

Do Not Track

All of the major web browsers support a feature called Do Not Track. With this option enabled, the browser sends a message to the web servers it communicates with saying "Do not track my usage." If the web server supports the Do Not Track feature, it will not store any information about the user's visit for analytics purposes, it will not attempt to place advertisers' cookies on the user's computer, and it will not place any scripts that attempt to track the user.

However, not every website supports the Do Not Track initiative. Compliance is optional, and there are no laws or rules requiring websites to support it. What this means is that even with the Do Not Track feature enabled, there is no way to know if the site you are visiting supports the Do Not Track feature. There are lists available that show supporting sites, but they change often. The website Donottrack.us maintains lists of supporting sites and networks, including advertising networks, at http://donottrack.us/implementations.

To enable the Do Not Track feature in Internet Explorer:

1. Click on the Settings button, then go to Safety.

2. From the menu that opens, click on or turn on Tracking Protection. Internet Explorer will open an add-on window.

3. From the window, click on Your Personalized List, then click on Enable at the bottom.

4. Close the window, then open it again.

Internet Explorer Add-On Window

5. The second time you open the add-on window, click on the option "Get a tracking protection list online." This opens a webpage where you can see a list of subscriptions you can install. The best option to start with is the EasyList Standard.

6. Right next to the EasyList Standard option, click on the Add button. This will bring up a confirmation box asking if you want to add the list to your browser.

7. Click on the Add List button.

8. To confirm or to add more subscriptions, open the add-on box by clicking on the Setting button, then on Manage Add-Ons.

9. On the left side, click on Tracking Protection.

10. To disable the Tracking option, click on the Settings button, then on Safety. The option to turn on tracking protection has changed to turn off tracking protection.

For Firefox:

1. Click on Settings, then on Options.
2. From the Options window, click on the Privacy tab.
3. At the top of the window in the Tracking section, click on the option to tell sites "I do not want to be tracked."

For Chrome:

1. Click on the Settings button, then on Settings.
2. From the Settings tab, click on the Show Advanced Settings option at the bottom. This will expand the Settings options to include more choices.
3. From this list, find the Privacy option and click on the box next to "Send a do not track request with your browsing traffic."

Browser Plug-Ins

One of the most efficient ways to control the way the browser operates on the Internet is to install plug-ins. Plug-ins can modify almost every part of the browser, changing how it functions and how it sends and receives information.

There are a variety of plug-ins that help safeguard privacy. Some of them block cookies or web bugs, others block advertising or social media scripts. Some plug-ins change the way the browser connects, or redirect traffic.

Installing Plug-Ins

Internet Explorer

To install plug-ins in Internet Explorer:

1. Start by opening the Add-Ons panel by clicking on the Settings icon, then clicking on Manage Add-Ons.

2. From the Add-On page, you will see a list of the different types of add-ons on the left side and the list of installed add-ons on the right side.

3. Make sure that the Toolbars and Extensions option is selected on the left side, and click on the option at the bottom of the page that says "Find more toolbars and extensions."

4. This opens the Internet Explorer Gallery where you can search for and find the extensions you want to install.

5. When you find the extension you want to install, click on the Add or "Add to Internet Explorer" button.

6. The browser will display a warning box at the bottom or top of the browser window asking if you want to run or save the file; or it will ask you if you want to add the extension to the browser.

7. If you are asked if you want to run or save it, choose Run; if you are prompted to add it, click the Add button.

8. It may then ask again if you want to install the extension; if it does, choose Install.

9. After installing, go back to the Manage Add-Ons page and verify that it was installed.

If you ever need to disable an add-on, you can do that from the Manage Add-Ons page by clicking on the extension and clicking on the Disable button at the lower right.

Firefox Add-On Window

Firefox

To access the add-ons for Firefox: Click on the Menu button, then click on the Add-Ons button.

This opens a new tab with several options on the left side. The first option, called "Get add-ons," displays a webpage where you can search for and find add-ons for Firefox. There are many types of add-ons available. They are sorted into categories including Appearance, Games, Privacy and Security, Search Tools, and Social and Communication. The next option is Extensions, where the list of currently installed extensions is provided. From this page, you can configure the settings for each extension and disable, enable, or remove installed extensions. The other options on the add-ons panel are the appearance add-ons where you can install themes, plug-ins that add functionality to the browser like Flash video or Java, and services like special add-ons from certain companies that add social features.

To find a specific add-on, browse the list of add-ons, or search using the Search box. Once you locate the add-on you want to install, click on the Install button on the Add-On page. The browser will download the add-on and install it. By default the browser will automatically install newer versions of installed add-ons. To change this behavior, from the Firefox Add-Ons page, click on the gear at the top of the page and uncheck the option "Update Add-Ons automatically."

If you want to disable or uninstall an add-on, from the Add-On page, click on the type of add-on you want to disable or delete on the left side—extension, appearance, plug-in, or service. From the list of add-ons on the right side, click on the option to either disable or remove the add-on. If you disable the add-on, it will stop functioning in the browser, and you can reenable it later.

Chrome

In Chrome, add-ons are called "extensions." To access the extensions:

1. Click on the Menu button, then on Settings.
2. On the left side, click on the option for extensions.

This will display a list of the currently installed extensions. To find extensions, click on the "Get more extensions" option at the bottom of the list of extensions. This will open a new tab to the Chrome web store. From this page, you can browse the list of extensions, or search for extensions using the search box on the upper left. As with Firefox, there are many types of extensions available. They are grouped into categories like Fun, Accessibility, Productivity, and Search Tools.

Chrome Extensions Window. Google and the Google logo are registered trademarks of Google Inc., used with permission.

Once you locate the extension you want to install:

1. Click on the button next to the extension that has a plus sign and a cost. Most of the extensions are free, but there are some that require you to purchase them. The browser will pop up asking you to confirm that you want to add the extension to the browser.

2. Click on the Add button to confirm it.

3. To confirm it was installed, go back to the Settings tab and click on Extensions. You should see it listed on the right side.

4. To disable an extension, uncheck the box next to the enabled option. If you want to remove an extension, click on the picture of the garbage can next to the extension you want to remove.

Plug-Ins or Extensions for Public Computers

There are many extensions that are used to protect users' privacy. The following list shows only a small percentage of the available extensions, but this is a great place to start. There are new extensions added every day. Recently, partially due to many high-profile incidents involving Internet privacy, there has been an upsurge in the number of privacy extensions available. Many of them offer the same basic protections like blocking cookies or automatically clearing the browser cache. The following extensions are ones that I have personally used or have researched their use, and they will work in a public computer situation.

Keep in mind that more is not always better. Several of these extensions block scripts, for example. Having more than one extension installed that all remove scripts can cause problems with the browser. It can also slow down the browser or cause instability. If you experience any issues browsing the Internet after extensions have been installed, try disabling the extensions. Start by disabling them all, then start reenabling them one at time in order to narrow down which one is causing the problems. Try different variations of types of extensions. If you have Disconnect .me and Adblock Plus installed on the same browser, and Adblock Plus is causing issues, try using Adblock Plus with Ghostery instead of Disconnect.me.

Disconnect.me

Disconnect.me is a browser extension available for Chrome, Firefox, Safari, and Opera. At this time they do not have a version for Internet Explorer. It blocks connections to other third-party web servers. It also blocks social media scripts to Facebook, Twitter, and Google Plus. Disconnect.me puts an icon on the toolbar of the browser that shows the user all the tracking requests that are currently on the page.

Disconect.me Toolbar Icon

To use Disconnect.me: After installing the extension, look for the D icon on the toolbar. While browsing the Internet, this icon lights up green and displays a number. The number that is displayed is the number of requests that Disconnect.me has blocked.

To view more information about the blocked requests, click on the D icon to drop down the interface. At the top of the window, there are three green boxes labeled F, G, and T. These are the requests to the social media sites Facebook, Google, and Twitter. If they are green, that means that the blocking is currently active; so if there are any requests to those sites, they will be blocked by Disconnect.me. The number to the right of the letter shows the number of requests to that social media site there are on that page.

To disable the blocking for that page, click on the letter icon. The box will turn grey, indicating that the blocking is turned off for that site. Below these boxes, there are four content request blocks, each one for a different category. The first is Advertising. This shows the number of requests to third-party sites that are categorized as advertisers. The next box down is Analytics. Analytics are requests made to third-party servers that are collecting data about the user for statistical purposes. The third one is Social. These

Disconnect.me Interface

are requests to other social networks besides the top three (Facebook, Google Plus, and Twitter). The last one is Content. These are requests made to third-party sites that are typically used like YouTube or Flickr. By default the Content option is disabled. You can tell if an option is disabled by whether it is grey, not green. To disable blocking for a category, or to turn it on, click on the icon for the category. That will turn the icon grey, and the page will reload, allowing those requests to be made. Each category can also be expanded to show more detail. Clicking on the right arrow next to the category will drop down the interface and show each individual site that is being blocked and how many requests were blocked for that site. Uncheck the box next to a particular site to unblock that request and allow it.

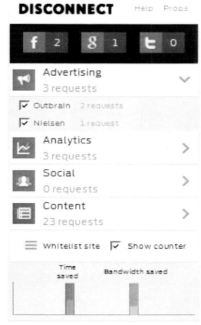

Disconnect.me Categories

Below the blocking categories, you'll see an option to "whitelist" the current site, which means it is cleared from blocking. Clicking on this option adds the current site to the whitelist, so Disconnect.me will no longer block requests for it. Once a site is on the whitelist, it has to be removed from the list to reenable blocking for it. If a site is on the whitelist, the option to whitelist the site changes to read "blacklist" site. Clicking on this removes the site from the whitelist, and Disconnect.me will start blocking third-party requests on that site again.

The "show counter" option turns off the visual display of how many requests were blocked. Below the whitelist and the counter option are three bar graphs showing different statistics regarding the blocking of the requests on the page. The first one on the left shows the amount of time that was saved by blocking the requests. Since the browser did not have to load and process all the requests, the page was displayed faster. If you hover your mouse over the graph, it will show how much faster it loaded. The next graph shows the amount of bandwidth that was saved. Bandwidth is the amount of data that was pulled down from the Internet. Since there were fewer requests made for data from other sites, there was a bandwidth savings. Hovering your mouse over the graph displays the amount saved. The last graph shows secured requests. According to the Disconnect.me site, it is no longer used and will be removed soon.

Adblock Plus

Disconnect.me does a great job of blocking requests, but it does not block all ads from displaying. Any ads that are generated by the site you are visiting will still be allowed to run and display. Another extension available for Internet Explorer, Firefox, and Chrome called Adblock Plus does a better job of hiding ads.

The extension works by subscribing to filter lists, which are lists of known ads. As a page is loaded, the extension compares all the links to the ads against its filter lists. If there is a match, the extension blocks that ad from displaying. By default, two lists are subscribed to when Adblock Plus is installed, a language-specific ad list and an acceptable ad list. The creators of Adblock Plus feel there are ads that are acceptable and that should be displayed to support the site operator. They compare the ad against the list, and if it matches one of the requirements for an acceptable ad, then the ad displays. For an ad to be considered acceptable by Adblock Plus, it must meet the following requirements:

- Ads must be static with no animations or sounds.
- Preferably, they are text only.
- They should never obscure page content, requiring the user to close the ad to view the page.
- All ads should be clearly marked with the word "advertising."

If an ad meets these requirements, it may be considered "acceptable" and will be displayed. If you want to remove the acceptable ads from the browser, you can remove that subscription.

To view, add, or remove Adblock subscriptions:

1. Open the Extension Configuration settings. For Chrome and Firefox, click on the red stop sign icon on the toolbar and choose Options.
2. From the Filter or Subscription List page, uncheck the box next to the subscription you want to disable, or click the red X, or drop down the Actions box to delete the subscription.
3. To subscribe to a new list, click on the Add Filter Subscription button.

4. Drop down the list of possible subscriptions and choose the one you want to add. Most of the subscriptions are for different countries or languages. The EasyList default subscription is adequate for most situations.

NoScript

NoScript, an extension available for Firefox, blocks all Javascript, Java, Flash, and other plug-ins from running on webpages by default. This is a very secure way of browsing since any plug-in or script that is launched on a site could be gathering personal information, browsing habits, and information about the user and sending it to online servers. Some scripts are potentially dangerous and allow hackers to place unwanted code on your computer. With NoScript, all forms of scripting and plug-ins are blocked by default, so you have to enable them for sites you want to allow scripts on. For example, if you were browsing a news site that had active content like videos or if you were using a site that had Javascript for applications or games, you would need to allow those scripts to run.

After installing NoScript, you will see the NoScript icon on the toolbar. The icon is the letter S. If there is a red circle with a line through the S, then that means the site has scripts on it that are blocked.

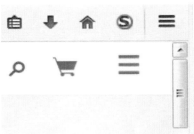

NoScript Toolbar Icon

If the S icon has a small red circle with a line through it, that means that the site has scripts on it that are not being blocked, but there are third-party scripts on the page that are being blocked.

If the icon is just an S without any additional icons on it, then all the scripts on the page are being allowed, and NoScript is not blocking anything.

NoScript Icon—No Blocking

As mentioned before, by default, NoScript blocks every script on a page. To allow scripts for a page:

1. Click on the S icon on the toolbar. This opens the NoScript interface.

2. From this interface, you can see all the sites that scripts are coming from and their status. Each section lists the site name and then two options. You can either allow the scripts from that site temporarily, or you can choose to allow the scripts for that site permanently. If a site is already allowed, then the option on the menu says "forbid."

3. To choose an option, click on it in the menu. After you do this, the site will reload and block the site, or allow it. If you choose to allow a site temporarily, then that site will be allowed for every site you visit until the browser is closed. Temporarily allowing scripts on a site is useful if you want to view a video, run an app, or perform some other activity on a site that does not work unless a script is allowed.

Temporarily allow cnn.com
Allow cnn.com

Temporarily allow postrelease.com
Allow postrelease.com

Temporarily allow clicktale.net
Allow clicktale.net

Temporarily allow optimizely.com
Allow optimizely.com

Temporarily allow outbrain.com
Allow outbrain.com

Temporarily allow turner.com
Allow turner.com

Untrusted ▶
Recently blocked sites ▶
Blocked Objects ▶

Temporarily allow all this page
Allow all this page
Allow Scripts Globally (dangerous)

Options...
About NoScript 2.6.9.13...

NoScript Main Interface

4. At the bottom of the menu, there are several more options. The first is an option called Untrusted with a menu attached to it. Choosing this option brings up a list of all the current sites that have scripts on the current page. From here you can mark any of the sites as untrusted. Some sites, like advertising sites, will show up in almost every list as having scripts. If you mark these sites as untrusted using this menu, they will not be displayed in the list of sites that can be allowed anymore. If a site is marked as untrusted, it can be marked as trusted again only from the untrusted menu.

5. The next option, Recently blocked sites, shows a list of the recent sites accessed and gives you the option to block or allow those sites. Below that is the option to allow all scripts on the current page until the browser is closed. Even further down there is the option to always allow all the scripts for the current page. The option below that allows all scripts for every site. This option basically disables most of the blocking features of NoScript.

There are several extensions for Chrome that have similar safety features. One of the most popular is called ScriptSafe.

ScriptSafe

ScriptSafe places an icon on the toolbar that looks like an exclamation mark if there are no scripts to block on the current page, or a red square with a white circle if there are scripts being blocked. Clicking on the icon shows the interface where you can choose to allow the scripts on the current page or deny them. You can also choose to trust the current site or distrust the site. At the bottom, you can choose to temporarily allow the scripts on the page.

ScriptSafe Interface

HTTPS Everywhere

HTTPS Everywhere is an extension for Firefox and Chrome that forces pages to load using an encrypted format. Using an encrypted format on pages prevents the data being transmitted between the server and client from being intercepted. The data is encrypted by the client and decrypted by the server, or encrypted by the server and decrypted by the client. Many servers support encrypted connections, but by default they use the unencrypted format. Using HTTPS Everywhere forces the client to request an encrypted page and use it if available.

The first time you launch the browser after you've installed this extension, it may ask you if you want to participate in the SSL Observatory. The SSL Observatory is an additional level of security that HTTPS Everywhere uses to make sure that the encryption certificates that the server uses are valid and not dangerous. Use of the SSL Observatory is optional. For public computers in a library, I do not recommend that you choose the option to participate in the SSL Observatory.

The HTTPS Everywhere icon is a small blue circle with a down arrow next to it. If the site you are viewing supports https, then the HTTPS Everywhere icon displays a number. The number shown is the number of first-party and third-party sites that were requested that support https. For example, on the Google.com homepage, the HTTPS Everywhere icon shows the number four. If you click on the icon, the HTTPS Everywhere interface drops down. On the interface, it shows the site that is using a secure connection and the status. If the site is green with a green checkmark, that means the site is using a secure connection, and it is

HTTPS Everywhere Interface

HTTPS Everywhere Interface
Showing Insecure Links

working correctly. If the site name is grey and there is a red X next to it, that means the site does not support secure connections. Even though the site you are connected to supports secure connections, all the other third-party servers that the server requests from may not support secure connections. This means that your communication to the primary server is encrypted, but your communication to the other third-party servers may not be.

Below the list of sites and their security status, you will see an option to disable HTTPS Everywhere. This turns off the extension, and all connections to servers will be unencrypted. The option below turns off the display showing how many sites are encrypted.

ZenMate Main Interface

ZenMate

ZenMate is an add-on for Firefox and Chrome that provides proxy-like services to the browser. When enabled, it directs all browser traffic through the ZenMate proxy. When it does this, it encrypts the data and strips out any identifying information in it. Your IP address while using ZenMate appears as a ZenMate IP address. Zen-Mate also attempts to identify and block potentially harmful sites. After ZenMate is installed and enabled, the icon on the toolbar looks like a green shield. If the icon is grey, then ZenMate is not enabled. Clicking on the icon drops down the ZenMate interface. If ZenMate is enabled, the interface shows privacy as protected. It also shows the path of your traffic. By default, ZenMate connects to the network in New York. This means that as you browse the Internet, your traffic appears to be coming from an IP address in New York. At the bottom of the interface, you can click on the Change Location option to have your traffic appear to originate from a different location. You can choose from New York, London, Frankfurt, Zurich, or Hong Kong.

Blur

Blur is a plug-in for all the major browsers including Internet Explorer, Firefox, and Chrome. Like other privacy plug-ins, Blur blocks browser scripts and web bugs that attempt to track you or gather information about you. It also adds additional services that include email masking for free. For an additional fee, they add even more services, including an online wallet to store masked credit card information, masked telephone numbers, and the ability to back up and synchronize your data across multiple devices.

The Blur icon is a blue circle with a white cross on it. If the application is currently blocking trackers, you will see a small green icon on it that shows the number of blocked trackers. Clicking on the icon opens the Blur interface. At the top of the interface, it shows the current site and how many trackers are blocked on it. Clicking on the option to show details opens yet another screen that shows what trackers were detected and their block status. You can allow a particular tracker by clicking on it. After enabling a tracker, you must manually reload the page for

Blur Interface

it to be enabled. Clicking on it again blocks it again. Below the list of blocked trackers is the option to disable the plug-in for the current site. Turning it off reenables all the trackers for that site until you block the site again. At the top of the tracker list is an option to view the tracking dashboard. The tracking dashboard is a webpage that shows the total number of trackers that have been blocked by your browser since the plug-in was installed. It also has a list of all the trackers that the plug-in

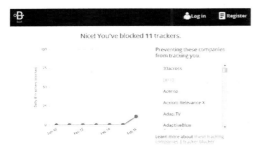

Tracking Dashboard

E-mail: *

Enter your email, then choose:

☑ Mask My Email   What is this?
☑ Use My Email
Ⓑ Blur   Settings   Help   Hide Panel

Password: *   Confirm Password: *

* Required Fields

Blur Sign-Up Page

recognizes and blocks. Some of the trackers are links that you can click on to learn more about the trackers.

By creating an account with Blur, you can get masked email addresses. Go to their website at http://www .abine.com/donottrackme.html, click on the sign-up link at the upper right, and create an account. Once the account is created, log into your account in the browser plug-in by opening the Blur interface and logging in. Now when you are on a site that requests an email address to create an account, you are given the choice of providing a masked email instead of your real email address. When you choose Mask My Email, the Blur application creates a one-time temporary email address that you use to sign up with. The Blur service then forwards the confirmation email you normally would have received from the website to your normal email account. From the point of view of the website, you have created an account, and your email address is the masked address. If they sell your email address or use it in any other way that you do not want them to do, they do not have access to your real email address. You can also disable or block the masked email address. This option is available at the top of every email that is sent to you from the masked address, and it is in the Blur interface. Click on Masking, then next to the option that says "Mask my email is on for this website," click on the On option to turn it off.

Lightbeam

Lightbeam is a tracker-visualizing plug-in for Firefox only. It monitors and watches the tracking information coming from websites and creates a visual representation of the connections between websites. It does this by gathering the cookies and other tracking scripts on webpages and making a list of them. As you browse the Internet, it continues to gather the tracking information and store it. When you open the Lightbeam interface, you are given a visual look at the sites you have visited and the trackers coming off them. To open the Lightbeam interface, click on the Lightbeam icon on the toolbar. From the Visual page, you can see the sites you visited as large circular icons with the graphic for the website you visited on it. Coming off these large circles are lines that represent the trackers for those sites. Triangle icons on the page show third-party tracker sites. The purple lines connecting the icons represent cookie files that were transferred. Clicking on a tracking icon triangle opens a side window with more information about that tracker. This includes the time and date of the accesses of that tracker, the location of the server, and what sites it is connected to.

Lightbeam Interface

Lightbeam itself does not at this time block any trackers or provide any protection from tracking. It is only a visualizing application. But it is very useful to see how the trackers are tracking you as you browse the Internet. On public computers, it would be useful to show patrons how the tracking works. It would also be useful for patron education sessions.

Since the browser is the primary way that patrons interact with the Internet, modifying it is the most effective and useful to way to help protect users' privacy. Enabling the privacy mode of the browser will help to keep the browser from keeping a history of the sites visited by other users of the computer. The Do Not Track initiative is useful for those sites that support it to prevent them from tracking users. Browser plug-ins or extensions provide easy ways to configure browsers to help provide privacy.

Bibliography

Abine. "Blur." Accessed December 20, 2014, https://www.abine.com/

Adblock Plus. Accessed December 20, 2014, https://adblockplus.org/

Disconnect. "Disconnect.me." Accessed December 20, 2014, https://disconnect.me/

Electronic Frontier Foundation. "HTTPS Everywhere." Accessed December 20, 2014, https://www.eff.org/https-everywhere

Google. "Chrome Incognito Mode." Accessed December 20, 2014, https://support.google.com/chrome/answer/95464

InformAction. "NoScript." Accessed December 20, 2014, http://noscript.net/getit

Mayer, Jonathan, and Arvind Narayanan. "Do Not Track." Accessed December 20, 2014, http://donottrack.us/

Microsoft. "Change Security and Privacy Settings for Internet Explorer." Accessed December 20, 2014, http://windows.microsoft.com/en-us/internet-explorer /ie-security-privacy-settings?ocid=IE_priv_browsing#ie=ie-11

Microsoft. "Use Tracking Protection in Internet Explorer." Accessed December 20, 2014, http://windows.microsoft.com/en-us/internet-explorer/use-tracking -protection#ie=ie-11

Mozilla. "Firefox Private Browsing Mode." Accessed December 20, 2014, https:// support.mozilla.org/en-US/kb/private-browsing-browse-web-without-saving -info?redirectlocale=en-US&as=u&redirectslug=Private+Browsing&utm _source=inproduct

Mozilla. "Lightbeam Visualizer." Accessed December 20, 2014, https://www.mozilla .org/en-US/lightbeam/

ZenMate. Accessed December 20, 2014, https://zenmate.com/

Index

About the Author

MATT BECKSTROM lives in beautiful Montana and works at the Lewis & Clark Library in Helena as the Systems Librarian. He has held this position since 1999. He has been using the Internet since 1992.

He received his bachelor's of science degree in Information Technology from Montana State University–Billings in 2009. He received his master's of information science degree with an emphasis on Information Systems from the University of North Texas in 2012.

He is active in the Montana Library Association, presenting frequently at conferences and serving on the board of directors.

He can be contacted at http://www.mattbeckstrom.com.